Reflections

on Automotive History

Bill Vance

Eramosa Valley Publishing

Canadian Cataloguing in Publication Data

Vance, Bill, 1935-
Reflections on automotive history

Collection of articles originally published in
The Toronto Star since 1986.
Includes index.

ISBN   0-9698922-0-9 (softcover edition)
       0-9698922-1-7 (hardcover edition)

1. Automobiles — History. I. Title.

TL15.V35 1994   629.222'09
C94-932460-4

Printed in Canada by
Ampersand Printing
123 Woolwich Street
Guelph, Ontario N1H 3V1
Telephone (519) 836-8800
Fax (519) 836-7204

Additional copies can be obtained from
Eramosa Valley Publishing
Box 370
Rockwood, Ontario, Canada
N0B 2K0

Cover photo by Richard Spiegelman.
Detail of 1937 Cord Supercharged 812

Pencil sketches by Hugh McCall.
Ford Model T
Volkswagen Beetle

TABLE OF CONTENTS

Foreword

Reflections on Automotive History is a collection of some of my columns that have appeared in *The Toronto Star* since 1986, and have been syndicated to other newspapers. As a student of the automobile, and particularly automotive history, it was difficult choosing from the more than 400 written. I naturally wanted to include every one. That of course was impossible, so those selected are a good representation of significant, interesting and unusual chapters in the 100-plus year history of the motor car.

This is not meant to be "heavy history," but rather, an easy and enjoyable read in which each chapter stands on its own. It is, on the other hand, still intended to be an accurate and informative chronicle of some of the vehicles, people and events that have made the automobile so significant in our society. There are chapters for every interest; family cars, sports cars and classic cars are all here.

This book is for the readers of my column. I have appreciated their kind words and encouragement, and have benefitted from their suggestions and ideas. I have also learned from and welcomed their corrections.

Constant readers may notice some differences between the chapters in the book and the columns as they originally appeared. This is because I have reviewed them all, and have often added to them by replacing material that had to be cut out by the editors due to space constraints.

As this is written, the column is being carried in Canada by the *Victoria Times-Columnist, Kelowna Daily Courier, Edmonton Journal, Moncton Times-Transcript, Fredericton Daily Gleaner, Halifax Chronicle-Herald, Old Autos,* and *The Toronto Star.* In the U.S. it runs in the *Atlanta Journal-Constitution* and the *Cleveland Plain Dealer.*

I wish to acknowledge the help of the automobile manufacturers and others who assisted with photos, particularly freelance photographer Richard Spiegelman. My eagle-eyed copy editor Richard Carroll also performed an invaluable service. I, of course, accept responsibility for any errors. Finally, I would like to thank the competent, friendly and patient folks at Ampersand Printing for guiding us through our first publishing effort. As noted, there are more than 400 columns, and counting, so we plan this as the first of a series.

Bill Vance
Rockwood, Ontario
November 1, 1994

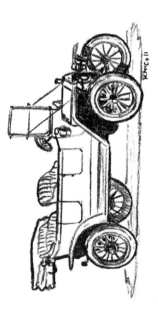

Ford Model T – Car of the Century

AMPHICAR

Every once in a while a glitch in the evolutionary process creeps in to upset orderly development and adaptation to an ever changing environment. Our subject is surely one of the more bizarre, for it's a vehicle that seems to be ambivalent about whether its natural environment is land or water.

The Amphicar aspires to be both a car and a boat. It is the embodiment of countless futuristic stories in such home handyman magazines as *Popular Science, Popular Mechanics* or *Mechanix Illustrated,* predicting ever more breathtaking breakthroughs in cars-as-boats, cars-as-planes, or even cars-as-helicopters. The Amphicar actually brought these fantasies down to earth (sea?) in the early 1960s in the form of an amphibious

Amphicar.

– EARL BRIMBLECOMBE

car. Leonardo da Vinci would have been proud. Inspiration for the German-built Amphicar is said to have come from the amphibious version of the World War II Volkswagen Kubelwagen, their "Jeep," known, appropriately enough, as the Schwimmwagen. In fact designer Hans Trippel reportedly had originally intended to use the VW drivetrain in the Amphicar, but marine regulations prohibited the use of an air-cooled engine.

After considering several alternatives, the best power-to-weight ratio compromise was found to be the British 1147 cc (70 cubic inch) overhead valve inline-four from the Triumph Herald. It developed a modest but adequate 43 horsepower at 4750 rpm, and was mounted in the rear of the vehicle behind the four-seater passenger compartment.

Industrie Werke Karlesruhe of West Berlin was formed in 1961 to manufacture Amphicars, which had to be capable of being licensed as both a car and a boat. Thus, in addition to the normal roadgoing requirements, they had to carry navigation lights, and such safety equipment as oars (fold-up types under the front seat), flares, lifejackets and a bilge pump. There was a lot of scepticism about the Amphicar's sea-going capability until a couple of Englishmen crossed the English Channel in one.

The performance of the Amphicar proved to be modest, whether on land or water. *Car and Driver* magazine tested one in November, 1967, and recorded a leisurely zero to 60 mph (96 km/h) time of 43 seconds, and estimated the top speed at 65 mph (105 km/h), when driving. As a boat they reported a top speed of six knots, or about 7 mph (11 km/h).

Amphicars never really caught on, either as cars or boats, with the result that they are rather scarce, although there is one in the Canadian Automotive Museum in Oshawa. A nice 1967 Amphicar, one of the last built, is also owned by Ken McGowen of Toronto, public spirited citizen and president of the Hasty Market chain of convenience stores.

On a recent clear fall afternoon Ken, aided by his son Dave who tends to the maintenance needs of the Amphicar, demonstrated its capabilities, and even gave me a turn at the wheel. It was a delightful experience.

On land the Amphicar rolls along with a kind of gentle rocking motion and is somewhat prone to wandering about; its aerodynamics are certainly not in the Mercury Sable class. The low gearing means that the little engine always seems to be churning out lots of revs to keep up with traffic. And while it may be capable of more than 60 mph (96 km/h) it definitely feels much more at home in the 40 to 45 mph (65 to 72 km/h) range, although Ken says he has seen 55 (88).

But one always has the impression that the Amphicar would rather be a boat, that it feels a little like, dare we say, a fish out of water when tooling through city streets. So we headed for a gently sloping stretch of beach on Humber Bay and prepared to take the plunge.

Changing the Amphicar from car to boat requires surprisingly little in the way of preparation. After securing the doors with the large handles at the lower rear corner of each door, the clutch is depressed and a small lever beside the main four-speed shifter is pushed forward to engage the twin nylon propellers. Following this, the car is put in first gear and driven straight into the water where the wheels keep it moving until it floats off the bottom and the propellers take over. First gear is then disengaged.

It's a surprisingly easy operation, yet one

approached with some trepidation by first timers because driving into the water is against all of the natural habits acquired over many years of driving. The first evidence that one is afloat is pure joy, almost disbelief.

One soon adapts to the change in status from driver to sailor as the Amphicar chugs along nicely at four or five knots. In spite of seeming to sit very low in the water, there is still about 20 inches (508 mm) of freeboard. There is no rudder so steering is accomplished in the water the same way it is on land - with the front wheels.

First time pilots, including this one, tend to flail away on the brake pedal, which of course does no good at all, except perhaps psychologically. A hand throttle is provided to relieve the strain on the right foot; cruise control in every sense of the word. Returning to terra firma is as easy as launching. One simply engages first gear again, drives out of the water, and disengages the propellers.

There is, however, one warning that I feel obliged to pass on. If you are a shrinking violet, have nothing whatsoever to do with the Amphicar because it attracts phenomenal attention. We were constantly getting waves, smiles, even looks of disbelief, particularly when in the Amphicar-as-boat mode.

Ken, and his good friend George Cohon, chairman of McDonald's Restaurants of Canada Ltd., who also has an Amphicar (Ken's plate

number is DRY WET and George's is WET DRY), have the right attitude. They regard their Amphicars as whimsical playthings and attention-getters.

After our afternoon splash we returned to Amphicar-as-car mode and motored up Toronto's Bay Street. True to the end to its offbeat character, the Amphicar emitted a very unladylike stream of water out of the rear (stern?) as the bilge pump did its necessary work.

AUSTIN-HEALEY

1956 Austin-Healey 100 with LeMans options.

— BILL VANCE

When Englishman Donald Mitchell Healey died in January 1988 at the age of 89, he left a lasting legacy in the many cars that bear his name. Although Healey had his own sports car company, the Donald Healey Motor Co. Ltd., Warwick, England, he seemed to spend more time building cars in co-operation with other manufacturers who wanted some of the Healey glamor.

Thus there was the Nash-Healey, the Austin-Healey Sprite, and the Jensen-Healey. But the car for which he will be best remembered is the big Austin-Healey, the "real" Healey to many, that was introduced as the Healey 100 in 1952, and quickly became the Austin-Healey 100.

Healey organized his car company right after World War II and built a variety of models in the late 1940s and early 1950s, none of which sold in great numbers. In 1950 he teamed up with the Nash Motor Co. of Kenosha, Wis., to design and build the Nash-Healey sports car, but it wasn't a commercial success either.

By 1951 it was apparent that North Americans were becoming enamored with English sports cars, the quintessential examples of which were the fast-selling MGs and Jaguars. But there was a huge price gap between the two, and late in 1951 Healey and his son Geoffrey set out to design a car priced to fit between the MG TD and the Jaguar XK120.

10

The Austin Motor Co. was approached and they were willing to sell the Healeys the 2.7 litre four-cylinder 90 horsepower engine, drivetrain, and suspension that they used in their Austin A-90 Atlantic sedan and convertible. The brakes and steering were also from Austin or its suppliers.

With the main components taken care of, the team then designed a sturdy twin-rail frame in which the side members were only 17 inches (432 mm) apart and joined by an X-section, which made it almost like a backbone type unit. A low-slung, simple yet stylish steel and aluminum roadster body was styled, riding on beautiful Rudge-Whitworth type wire wheels with knock-off hubs. The Healey 100 had been born.

The Healey 100 made its public debut at the London Motor Show in the fall of 1952 and was an immediate sensation. When Leonard Lord, head of the British Motor Corp. (BMC) that had just been formed through the merger of Austin and Morris, saw the 100 he knew he had to have it. A deal was struck with Healey and two days later the car sported an Austin-Healey badge.

The Austin-Healey 100 went into production in 1953 and began to arrive in North America in quantity late in the year. The established BMC dealer network provided a ready-made distribution system.

To give the new car a publicity boost, and prove the durability of the Austin long-stroke engine (bore and stroke were 3.44 by 4.38 inches,

or 87.4 by 111.1 mm), an Austin-Healey was taken to the International Record Trials held on the Bonneville Salt Flats in Utah in September, 1953.

By the end of the trials there wasn't much doubt about the Austin-Healey's durability and performance. It broke more than 100 class D (cars with engines of 2.0 to 3.0 litres of displacement) records, and shattered all American stock car records for distances from five to 3000 miles.

To prove its durability, a stock Austin-Healey averaged 104 mph (167 km/h) for 30 hours, and as far as top speed was concerned, a modified Healey achieved 142.6 mph (230 km/h) in a one-mile, two-way average.

When it got into the hands of the testers, the Healey's numbers weren't quite as spectacular, although they were still very respectable. *Road & Track* magazine tested one in their July, 1954, issue and reported a top speed average of 102.3 mph (165 km/h) and a zero to 60 mph (96 km/h) time of 11.7 seconds, not all that far off the 10.1 seconds it had recorded for the Jaguar XK120. The Austin-Healey was very close in performance to its Triumph TR2 rival, which had a zero to 60 (96) time of 12.2 and top speed of 103 (166).

The Austin-Healey was fitted with a three-speed manual transmission (an Austin four-speed with first gear blocked out), but because it had overdrive, which could be actuated in second and third gears, it had the equivalent of a five-speed gearbox. Third-overdrive was a long-legged ratio that allowed the big four to loaf along at 2500 rpm at 60 mph (96 km/h), and helped to compensate for that ancient long-stroke design.

The 100 sold well and continued in production until 1956, with a higher performance model, the 100S (100 for horsepower; S for Sebring), as well as a four-speed gearbox, being added along the way. In 1956 BMC announced that it would be discontinuing the big four, so the Healeys modified the car to accept the Austin A-105 2.6 litre overhead valve inline six cylinder engine.

This resulted in a car, the 100-Six, that had, as *Road & Track* said in its January, 1957, road test: "Two more cylinders, two more seats, two more wb (wheelbase) inches, two more mph." The addition of the two inches (51 mm) to the wheelbase to bring it to 92 inches (2337 mm), helped accommodate the longer engine, and moving the spare tire into the trunk made possible the fitting of two tiny optional seats in the rear. A new oval-shaped grille was fitted but, in the opinion of many, it lacked the distinctiveness of the triangular original.

Despite the more powerful 102 horsepower six, the new car was a little slower in acceleration than the 100, with a zero to 60 mph (96 km/h) time of 12.2 seconds. This was no doubt due to its weight gain from 2150 to 2480 pounds (976 to 1125 kg). Top speed was now 105 mph (169 km/h).

For 1959 the Austin-Healey evolved into its final version with the introduction of the 3000 model. Its six-cylinder engine had been bored out to yield 2912 cc and horsepower was up to 136, which dropped the zero to 60 (96) time down to 9.8 seconds and increased the top speed to 112 mph (180 km/h).

This model went through Mark I, Mark II, Mark II convertible, and Mark III versions before production ceased in 1967, the victim of U.S. safety and emissions legislation.

Big Austin-Healeys were sturdy and enjoyable cars and there are many of the 71,568 that were produced still being driven by happy owners.

There were a few disadvantages, of course, such as some transmission problems, electrolytic corrosion due to the mating of dissimilar body metals, and the notoriously low ground clearance that kept Healey drivers on a sharp lookout for curbs and anything taller than a golf ball, although the Mark IIIs were somewhat better in this respect. But muffler shops have to make a living too. In spite of a few shortcomings Austin-Healeys are fondly remembered and eagerly collected sports cars.

DAIMLER AND BENZ

Originators of the Automobile

The modern automobile is a marvel of technical efficiency. It is smooth, powerful and clean, and relative to a few years ago, quite economical. And it has all come through an evolution covering just over 100 years.

The first practical recognized internal combustion engine powered cars were invented by two German engineers named Karl Benz and Gottlieb Daimler. They were born 10 years apart - Daimler in 1834, and Benz in 1844 - in Southern Germany. Although they lived only 100 kilometres (62 miles) apart, and their companies would ultimately merge, they never met. Their pioneering vehicles would appear within one year of each other, with Benz the first to be

Karl Benz's first car (left) and Gottlieb Daimler's (right).
— BILL VANCE

granted a patent on his three-wheeled Benz "Patent Motorwagen" on January 29, 1886.

Daimler began working in his teens for a heavy machinery manufacturer that made bridges, railway cars and locomotives, and was able to study engineering at Stuttgart Polytechnikum. He was, however, unenthusiastic about steam engines. He was more interested in the new internal combustion engines from such inventors as a Belgian named Jean-Joseph Lenoir, and later from Nicholas Otto, in collaboration with Eugene Langen. He dedicated himself to learning everything he could about them.

In 1872 Daimler took over the management of Gasmotoren-Fabrik Deutz, manufacturer of

13

obtain sufficient financial backing to begin manufacturing his two-stroke engine in Mannheim. It became Gasmotorenfabrik Mannheim in 1882, but Benz departed shortly after due to a difference of opinion with his partners; he wanted to go into road vehicles and they didn't. Benz was able to find backers and opened his own company, Benz & Cie., to build gas engines, quietly starting to make a four-stroke design in 1884.

In the meantime Daimler and Maybach worked feverishly at improving the four-stroke engine by reducing weight and increasing speed. Also, a waste product called benzine (petrol in Britain; gasoline in North America) resulting from the distillation of mineral oil from the recently drilled oil wells, was found to be a suitable fuel. It would allow engines to be mobile, freeing them from the town coal-gas mains.

Benz too was working on a smaller, lighter version of his engine. Igniting the benzine was a very difficult problem, but Benz finally figured out how to fire the mixture using a battery with a coil and spark plug. It was an ingenious and important breakthrough in the development of the internal combustion engine.

With a usable engine, Benz now began to create a vehicle for it to power. After considering three and four wheels, he decided on a three-wheeler, probably because he didn't know how to build a steering system for two front wheels.

the Otto and Langen two-stroke internal combustion engine. While Daimler managed the plant, Otto worked on improving the engine. The breakthrough came in 1876 when he completed his four stroke - intake, compression, power and exhaust - design. This was patented in 1877 as the "Otto-cycle" engine. Compressing the coal gas mixture in the engine proved more efficient in extracting the energy from it, and Daimler immediately set the Deutz plant to work manufacturing the new type of powerplant.

Daimler and Otto were strong-willed men, so strong that it became impossible for them to continue working for Deutz. Since Otto held the patent, Deutz fired Daimler. He then moved to Canstatt, near Stuttgart, and with the very able assistance of Wilhelm Maybach, also from Deutz, opened his own machine shop in a converted greenhouse in 1882.

After graduating in engineering from Karlsruhe Polytechnikum Karl Benz had also gone into steam engine work. He then changed to building weigh scales, and finally into bridge design. Like Daimler, however, he was keenly interested in internal combustion engines. Since Otto held the four-stroke patent, although it would ultimately be declared void in 1886, Benz concentrated on the two-stroke design, which accomplished the operating cycles in two strokes of the piston, or one crankshaft revolution.

He found success in 1879, and was able to

His first "car" therefore, was a light, two-passenger tricycle-type vehicle with two large spindly wire-spoked wheels driven by a chain at the rear, and a smaller tiller-steered one in front. It was strongly influenced by bicycle technology.

The one-cylinder engine was mounted horizontally behind the seat. Its first test drive was in the fall of 1885 on Benz's property. After receiving his patent in January 1886, he risked slightly longer trips, but never too far for Karl and his son Eugene to push the little car back home. These tests were made at night to avoid the embarrassment of breakdowns. Finally in July 1886, he made a successful test drive around the perimeter of Mannheim.

But Benz was never satisfied, and while he continued tinkering, his wife Bertha grew more and more impatient. She had worked with him in the development of the car, and she believed it should now be tested over a longer distance. Finally she and her two sons stole out early one morning and set out for Pforzheim, some 80 kilometres (50 miles) away. They made the trip successfully, albeit with the boys pushing up the hills, and proved that the little Benz was a practical road car. Karl's response is unrecorded, but he was probably secretly proud of both his car and his wife.

As Benz was building his car, Daimler had experimented with his engine in a motorcycle and a boat. He then ordered a sturdy carriage, keeping his real purpose secret by saying it was for his wife's birthday. He fitted his engine to it, and the four-wheeler was test driven successfully in the fall of 1886.

Daimler and Benz would both establish successful automobile companies, which would join in 1926 to form Daimler Benz, manufacturer of Mercedes-Benz motor vehicles. Gottlieb Daimler died in 1900 and Karl Benz in 1929, their places in history secure as the inventors of the machine that would change the world.

BMC Mini/Mini-Coopers

BMC Mini.

— BILL VANCE

When the British Austin/Morris Mini came on the scene in 1959, and the American Pontiac Tempest in 1961, they had something in common: both had unusual drivetrains. The Mini's cross-mounted engine and front drive layout was the more brilliant stroke, and would set the direction for much of the automotive world. But the Tempest, although not as radical, was still out of the mainstream, especially for North America, with its "hanging rope" driveshaft, rear-mounted transaxle and half-a-V-8 four-cylinder engine.

Something else the cars had in common was that they would go on to form the basis for high-performance sedans, the quintessential muscle cars of their respective countries.

Pontiac V-8 into the light intermediate Tempest for 1964 (the odd driveshaft and rear transmission were now gone) and called it the GTO.

The Mini also gained its fame from having more displacement than the standard model, although on a somewhat smaller scale. It was designed in the 1950s by Alec Issigonis, a no nonsense, autocratic British Motor Corp. engineer; with the Mini he would be one of the last people to personally create a whole car.

The Mini's genesis could be traced back to the brief 1956 Middle East war when Egypt's Gamal Abdel Nasser closed the Suez Canal and seemed

The Pontiac gained its notoriety when Pontiac engineers dropped a big 389 cubic inch (6.4 litre)

16

about to precipitate a full-scale oil shortage. BMC's head, Sir Leonard Lord, wanted a really economical car to conserve fuel and to drive off the streets what he considered those horrid little "bubble cars" like Isettas and Messerschmitts.

Issigonis's mandate was that everything could be new except the engine, which must be an existing BMC unit. He and his crew went to work and in less than 18 months had a prototype Mini to demonstrate to Sir Leonard. Lord was delighted and ordered production to begin within a year. The Austin/Morris Mini was introduced to the public in the summer of 1959.

It was a truly novel design, the ultimate in space utilization, comprised as it was of just two boxes: one for the drivetrain and the other for passengers and luggage.

Placing the engine crosswise, sharing the engine sump with the transmission, and driving the front wheels yielded the most compact driveline possible. Tiny 10-inch wheels and rubber cone suspension (later replaced by a more sophisticated interconnected front to rear "Hydrolastic" type) instead of coil springs, encroached very little on interior space.

The result was a car that could carry four passengers and a reasonable amount of luggage within only a 10-foot (3048 mm) overall length and an 80-inch (2032 mm) wheelbase. And it provided a ride that was, if not plush, at least tolerable.

17

While Issigonis disdained styling, regarding it as a tool of obsolescence, the Mini nevertheless had a basic, functional cuteness that was appealing almost in spite of itself.

Another attribute was excellent handling. The car's small size, of course, made it very manoeuvrable and easy to park, but the Mini also stuck to the corners like glue. This soon prompted motoring's sportier elements to seek more performance than the tiny 850 cc engine's 37 horsepower could provide. It attracted the attention of one John Cooper, engine tuner and race car builder par excellence (he had two Formula 1 constructor's championships to his credit).

Cooper was an old friend of Issigonis, and while the car's creator was initially cool toward the idea of a faster Mini, he soon agreed to team up with Cooper to give the Mini more muscle. The result was the Mini-Cooper of 1961 powered by a 55-horsepower, 998 cc twin-carburetor engine that raised top speed from 75 to 85 mph (121 to 137 km/h).

The Mini-Cooper delighted the motoring press, turned Issigonis into a performance enthusiast, and found immediate favor with the competition community, particularly rallyists. It was a car that was so easy to drive quickly that average motorists were soon embarrassing the owners of much more expensive sports cars; they found those little gnats extremely difficult to shake off.

In that old Detroit idiom that if big is good,

bigger must be better, work was begun on building an even faster Mini, and the Mini-Cooper S of 1963 was the result. It was initially intended to be for competition only and came in engine displacements of 970, 1071 and 1275 cc. But the S was so good that customer demand dictated that it be offered to the public. The 1275 cc version became the production model.

To say that the Mini-Cooper S was a sensation would be an understatement. Here was a little car that could be flung around corners, could (according to a *Road &Track* test of November, 1965) sprint to 60 mph (96 km/h) in 10.5 seconds, and reach a top speed of 98 mph (158 km/h). It became an overnight success in rallying and sedan racing.

The S dominated European rallying until the late '60s, with Paddy Hopkirk, one of the fastest Mini pilots, winning the prestigious Monte Carlo Rally four times, 1964 through '67, although he was denied '66 due to a lighting infraction.

Hopkirk was so entranced with the car that he later went into the business of making what he called replicas (not really replicas as they were rebuilt pre-66s). He hung a name on his version that was practically longer than the car: Paddy Hopkirk Mini-Cooper S Works Replica.

The S was also the weapon of choice in sedan racing, cornering at lurid angles while it outran bigger and allegedly faster cars.

With the introduction of the heavier Mark II Mini of 1968, the S lost some of its edge. Also, the competition was getting much stronger by this time.

The Mini-Cooper S continued in production until 1971, and it is still raced, rallied and loved by enthusiasts to this day. Like those early Pontiac GTOs, it is now a sought-after collectible.

18

BMW Isetta

There we were, a couple of guys just trickling through Toronto's trendy Yorkville in our BMW. Nothing unusual about that you might say. BMWs, Jaguars, Mercedes-Benzes, Porsches and their ilk are as common in Yorkville as ants at a picnic. Why then were we attracting so many stares, smiles, questions, and yes, even a wink or two? Well, I have to admit that it wasn't our charisma; it was the car. You see, this was no regular, run-of-the-mill big-bucks Bimmer. This was a tiny BMW Isetta 300, egg-shaped progeny of Italian creativity and German motorcycle engineering.

Bubble cars came onto the European auto scene in the '50s in response to high gasoline

1959 BMW Isetta 300.

– Howard Lipton

prices, and the simple need for weather-proof, personal transportation, no matter how basic. It was a step up from a motorcycle and sidecar.

In 1952 an Italian refrigerator manufacturer, Renzo Rivolta of Milan, decided to get into the car business. His fridges carried the Iso brand name so he called his little vehicle the Isetta, literally "small Iso."

The Isetta, introduced in 1953, set the whole bubble car trend in motion. The most striking features, once one got past the egg-inspired shape, was the method of entry and exit. Perhaps Rivolta was inspired by his refrigerators when he designed it because the entire front of the car, including the windshield, is a door that swings out, bringing the universal-jointed steering column with it. Occupants step aboard and sit down and the driver pulls the steering wheel back to close the door, which is then latched manually.

The 47-inch (1194 mm) front track was about normal for a small car of that era, but the mere 20 inches (508 mm) between the rear wheels was decidedly unusual. It did, however, eliminate the need for a differential; a chain transmitted the power from the engine to a large sprocket attached to the drive axle in the rear housing. The Isetta was powered by a 236 cc two-stroke, two-cylinder air-cooled engine mounted just ahead of the right rear wheel, the location chosen to counterbalance the weight of the driver. The four-speed transmission was shifted by a lever with an "upside-down H" pattern, located to the left of the driver.

Rivolta built the Isetta until 1955, when he decided to stop. He would return to car building in 1962 with vehicles at the other end of the spectrum: high powered sports cars called Iso Rivoltas.

At about the time Rivolta was abandoning car building, the German auto and motorcycle manufacturer, BMW, was undergoing financial difficulties. Its luxurious, expensive six-and eight-cylinder cars weren't selling well, and motorcycle sales had softened seriously. BMW had to do something, so in order to get into the affordable bottom end of the car market, BMW bought the rights to the Isetta.

BMW replaced the two-stroke engine with a modified version of one of its motorcycle engines, an air cooled 247 cc single-cylinder four-stroke that developed 12 horsepower. A 295 cc 13 horsepower engine would be added in 1956 for the export models, which gave the Isetta its 300 name. BMW also fitted a more conventional trailing arm and coil spring front suspension in place of the horizontal coils used by Iso.

The Isetta sold well enough that BMW could afford to expand the line with a four passenger version in 1957. It was called the 600 after its flat, 585 cc, 19.5 horsepower two cylinder motorcycle engine. The 600 retained the front opening door and added a right rear side door for access to the surprisingly roomy back seat. Transmission shifting was through a more conventional four-on-the-floor lever.

Isettas were also built under licence in France, Brazil and England. Total production between 1955 and 1962 was almost 162,000 in the bubble window, sliding window, and convertible versions. There was even a rare pickup truck.

The performance of the Isetta could best be described as marginal, and it was definitely not freeway friendly. Road & Track magazine tested one in its February, 1958 issue and recorded a top speed of approximately 50 mph (80 km/h) and a zero to 40 mph (64 km/h) acceleration time of 20 seconds. Fuel economy was tremendous, however, being in the 60 to 75 mpg range.

Howard Lipton of Toronto, the local representative of the Microcar and Minicar Club in the U.S. (formerly the Heinkel-Messerschmitt-Isetta Club of America) is not only a guru of Isetta-ology, but is also the proud owner of a 300 and a 600, both 1959s, and both in excellent condition. He was kind enough to give me a ride-and-drive demonstration in them.

Entry is simply a matter of opening the wide door and stepping in. The Isetta engine spins smoothly thanks to the combination generator-starter "Dynastart," and fires up quickly. One is immediately aware that it's a one-lunger because of the vibration and noise. First gear is a little balky, but once underway the tiny vehicle at least feels fast, thanks to the high-revving engine. The left handed, backward shift pattern is soon mastered and by rowing the lever, the driver can usually keep up with normal traffic.

Visibility is excellent, akin to living in a fishbowl, and this turns out to be an important feature. One soon learns to scan the road for large potholes that would swallow the tiny 10-inch wheels, and for large vehicles (they are *all* larger) that would threaten the safety of the tiny car and its passengers. Parking, of course, is a breeze; simply nose into the curb and step out onto the sidewalk.

Riding in an Isetta is not for the shy or retiring

because the car attracts attention everywhere it goes. Howard had to resort to having information sheets printed so he could hand them out and escape endless questions. The most often heard enquiry? Is this really a BMW? Many people apparently missed this short chapter in BMW history.

The Isetta and the 600 helped BMW pull back from the brink of bankruptcy. It introduced a 700 model in 1960, a more conventional appearing car, although still powered by a rear-mounted air-cooled twin. The big break came in 1962 with the launching of the 1500, forerunner of the very successful 2002.

BRICKLIN

1975 *Bricklin.*

The similarities between Malcolm Bricklin and John DeLorean are inescapable. Both were high-flying promoters who tried to be the first man to launch a North American-based automobile company since Preston Tucker's attempt back in the 1940s. Both went into high unemployment areas and convinced desperate and gullible governments to sink millions in public money into dubious enterprises. Both would run afoul of the law during their careers. Both seemed to have delusions of grandeur. And both even insisted that their cars have gull-wing doors.

There were differences too, of course. DeLorean was a seasoned automotive engineer whose accomplishments with General Motors Corp. brought him to the position of group executive, and in contention for the presidency, at the relatively young age of 48.

Bricklin, on the other hand, had dropped out of his first year at the University of Florida where he joked about majoring in "time and space." His automobile knowledge was in about the same category.

But he had drive, and by the time he was 25 Bricklin had parlayed the family building supply business into a franchised chain of Handyman hardware stores in the U.S. He sold the business in 1964 amid a flurry of lawsuits, claiming to have made a million dollars.

His next enterprise was marketing a ware-

22

house full of Lambretta motor scooters that lay stockpiled unsold in Philadelphia. This led to selling motor scooters made by Fuji Heavy Industries of Japan, who also happened to make an extremely basic mini-car called the Subaru 360.

Bricklin convinced Fuji that he and a partner, Harvey Lamm, could market the car in the U.S. He knew that since the 360 weighed less than 1000 pounds (454 kg), it wasn't considered a car by the U.S. government, and thus was immune from automobile safety regulations.

Sales of the 360 went well for a while, until Consumer Reports magazine called it the most unsafe car in the U.S. Exit Mr. Bricklin in 1971, again with allegations of wrongdoing, to set up his General Vehicle Corp. in Scottsdale, Ariz. for the purpose of building his own car. Bricklin engaged a California custom car builder to produce a prototype. Although he had originally planned to use a four-cylinder engine, American Motors had a supply of 360 cubic inch (5.9 litre) V-8s available, so a deal was made for them.

The prototype was marginally engineered, but ran well enough for the shooting of a short film that Bricklin used to promote the car. He called it the Bricklin SV-1 (for safety vehicle, another DeLorean similarity). It had its exotic gull-wing doors and was good enough to convince several banks, the biggest of which was the First Pennsylvania, to invest close to a million dollars in the enterprise.

While a small shop was set up in Livonia, Mich., to develop the prototype for production, Bricklin hit the road with his film and his charisma; he was out to sell his dream. His goal was to find a factory in which to build his car, a search that led him to Canada.

Bricklin joined forces with Jack Reese who had been a sales executive with Renault Canada, which was closing its St. Bruno, Que., assembly plant. They were able to pre-sell a number of Bricklin franchises, and obtain orders for 2000 cars.

Thus encouraged, Malcolm contacted the government of Quebec about acquiring the St. Bruno plant; if Quebec would lend him $7 million, Bricklin would give them a 40 percent interest in the company. While interested in getting the plant back into production, Quebec was also cautious.

It asked Jean de Villers of Renault, who was looking after the disposal of the plant, to visit Philadelphia and investigate Bricklin. De Villers reported that Bricklin was a high liver, possessing, among other things, a Rolls-Royce, a Corvette, and a Lamborghini. He was a good promoter, but not a very good manager. Quebec said no thanks to Bricklin's deal.

Bricklin's next stop was New Brunswick, which eventually led to the office of then-premier Richard Hatfield. Hatfield saw the film and was captivated by the idea of a New Brunswick-produced car; a deal was struck in which the province would provide loan guarantees of $2.88 million, and purchase 51 percent of Bricklin Canada's shares for $500,000.

A plant was found in Saint John, although it would prove too small to assemble the entire car, so an additional facility in Minto would be used to produce the glass fibre-backed acrylic-skinned bodies.

By August, 1974, 200 dealers had been signed up, ironically all in the U.S. because, since Bricklin could not gain access to the Auto Pact, he could not sell his cars in Canada. Production of sorts was also getting under way in Saint John.

There were real problems, however, because the car was still under-engineered, and the acrylic-covered bodies being made in Minto were of poor quality. In addition, a large percentage of the body panels were damaged enroute to Saint John.

What was to be the Bricklin's crowning styling touch, the gull-wing doors, were a disaster that the engineers worked mightily to overcome. They were heavy (90 pounds; 41 kg), slow to open, subject to leaks, and in the event of an electrical failure, the occupants had to exit through the rear hatch. It would not be a very elegant way to arrive at the opera.

General assembly quality was poor and the bodies were subject to cracks and scratches, although light surface imperfections could be buffed out. The pop-up headlights often didn't pop up, and windshields would leak.

The end finally came in September, 1975, when the company was placed in receivership. New Brunswick had stopped the infusion of cash at $23 million, a staggering amount for a province that was suffering high unemployment. The best estimate is that 2857 Bricklins were produced.

Back in the U.S., Malcolm Bricklin went on to other enterprises such as importing Fiat X1/9s badged as Bertones, and then organizing Global Motors to distribute the Yugo car from Yugoslavia.

Ettore Bugatti

Automotive history is liberally sprinkled with bizarre and unusual characters, men of strong will, unbounded vision, questionable ethics, or hopeless conservatism. The Billy Durants, Henry Fords, André Citroëns, Karl Benzes, Ferdinand Porsches, Preston Tuckers, John DeLoreans, Enzo Ferraris and Lee Iacoccas have left their indelible marks on the automobile world.

But none has bequeathed a more lasting legacy of eccentric behavior and unusual yet revered motor cars than Ettore Bugatti. Bugatti was born in Milan, Italy, in 1881, although he lived almost all of his life in France. He began to take an interest in motor vehicles in his teens, entering several races and becoming a proficient driver. There was

Bugatti Type 35B 1926 GP car.

— Bill Vance

also a creative talent in him and he considered being an artist.

When it became apparent that his brother Rembrandt possessed greater artistic talent, he abandoned the idea; it was not Ettore Bugatti's nature to be second best.

His artistic and mechanical abilities were soon to become apparent to the automobile world when, in 1901, a car he designed won a gold medal at the International Exhibition in Milan. This attracted the attention of one Baron de Dietrich who invited Bugatti to design cars for him. These were called De Dietrich-Bugattis, and this association lasted until 1904 when the two men came to a parting of the ways.

Bugatti then worked as a designer for the

25

Mathis auto company of Strasbourg, France, until joining Deutz in 1907 as chief designer when that company decided to get into the automobile business. Gasmotorenfabrik Deutz had a proud engine building heritage, being the company that manufactured the first successful gas engine. The engine had been invented by Nicolaus August Otto, but Deutz had not yet used it in cars.

Although working for others, Bugatti harbored a desire to build his own car and in fact had been laying down the design for one in his basement. In 1909 he was fortunate enough to find a banker by the name of de Viscaya who would back him financially.

An abandoned dye works was found near Strasbourg in Molsheim, Alsace-Lorainne (now BasRhin), and Automobiles E. Bugatti was established with a staff of three. The small company managed to build three cars during 1910, and by 1911 had grown to a staff of 65. One of the original three men, master mechanic Ernest Friederich, was also an excellent racing driver and entered a Type 13 Bugatti in the 1911 LeMans Grand Prix.

At a mere 330 kg (727 pounds), it was by far the lightest car in the race, so light in fact that it had to run in the open class because it didn't weigh enough to qualify for the light car class. It was powered by an overhead cam four cylinder engine that was, at 1.3 litres, tiny by the standards of the period.

It would prove to be a significant event. Al-

though Friedrich didn't win the race, he did perform a giant-killing feat by coming in second, beating the entire field with the exception of a huge Fiat.

It was a powerful straw in the wind, an indication that small, good handling cars with high-revving engines would soon spell the end to the huge-displacement monsters then being campaigned in Grand Prix races.

The racing success gave the young company overnight credibility, and while Bugatti wouldn't return to racing for 11 years, the enterprise was successful in spite of an interruption during World War I (1914-1918) when the Germans occupied the plant. Thankfully, it wasn't damaged and Bugatti was able to resume production in 1919.

In all, Bugatti produced about 50 models, or Types, as he called them, with the two most famous probably being the Type 35 and Type 41.

The Type 35 appeared in 1924 and was produced in both racing and touring forms. It was a spare design that was beautifully proportioned from its inverted horseshoe-shaped radiator and narrow hood, to its pert boat-tailed rear end. It was an immediate success and Bugattis would go on to win a record-breaking 1800-plus races in the 1924-27 period.

The Type 41, the Bugati Royale, was at the other end of the automotive spectrum from the Type 35. While the 35 was small, efficient and lean, the Royale was huge, ostentatious and expensive. It had a wheelbase of 168.1 inches (4270 mm), weighed some 7000 pounds (3176 kg), and was powered by a 12.8 litre (779 cubic inch) overhead cam inline eight-cylinder engine that developed 300 horsepower. It was launched in 1929 and Bugatti had planned a production run of 25 cars, although only six (possibly seven, experts disagree) were ever built.

Ettore Bugatti had intended the car for royalty, hence the name. Ironically, no royalty ever bought one. It almost happened though, and the fact that it didn't gives some insight into the sensitivities of Bugatti.

An Albanian monarch visited Bugatti's chateau in Molsheim for the purpose of purchasing a Type 41. Among other things Bugatti observed what he considered to be unacceptable table manners.

When the visit was being concluded and the king inquired about when he might be able to obtain a Royale, he was advised that none was available, and, unfortunately, the factory could not say when they could build one.

On another occasion Bugatti encountered a customer at the factory with a troublesome car. "You, monsieur, I think, are the one who has brought his Type 46 back three times," said Bugatti. The man replied that he was, confident that things would finally be put right. "Do not let it happen again," Bugatti replied imperiously.

The best years for the Bugatti company were prior to 1929. They were hurt by the Great Depression as were other motor manufacturers, and, of course, production stopped during World War II. Only half-hearted attempts were made to resume post-war production. Two Bugatti Grand Prix cars were built in 1956, and the marque has recently been revived again as an exotic supercar powered by a turbocharged V-12. Only time will tell whether this attempt to bring back the fabled automotive name will be successful.

Ettore Bugatti died in 1947, a year that also claimed two other automotive legends, Henry Ford I, and Billy Durant, founder of General Motors.

Despite his idiosyncrasies, Ettore Bugatti left us some rare and almost priceless motorcars. Of the 7500 Bugattis built, an amazing 1200 are said to still exist. A Bugatti Royale is on display in the Henry Ford Museum in Dearborn, Mich.

BUICK'S 90TH ANNIVERSARY

Buick marked its 90th anniversary in 1993, making it one of the oldest and most respected automobile nameplates in the world. And in those nine decades Buick was touched by many of the great pioneers of the automotive industry, men like William (Billy) Durant, founder of GM, Walter Chrysler, Louis Chevrolet, the famous race driver who gave his name to Chevrolet, and Charles Nash, the father of the Nash Motor Co.

Buick's roots can be traced back to Scotland where David Dunbar Buick was born on Sept. 17, 1854. Brought to the United States when he was just two, David Buick grew up to become a successful Detroit plumbing contractor and innovator, his most

1905 Buick.

– BILL VANCE

famous invention being a method for making porcelain adhere to iron plumbing fixtures.

In the late 1890s Buick became interested in something more exciting than plumbing: gasoline engines. He organized the Buick Auto-Vim and Power Co. in 1899, the Buick Manufacturing Co. in 1902, and finally, the Buick Motor Co. in May, 1903. These firms produced a couple of experimental cars and a variety of boat and stationary farm engines.

The invention that would set Buick on its way to fame, however, was the valve-in-head engine. Developed by Buick's chief engineer Walter Marr, and engineer Eugene Richard, the light, powerful engine proved to be more efficient

28

than the side-valve designs then in general use. But Buick didn't have the capital to exploit the overhead-valve design, so the company was sold to the Flint Wagon Works in 1903, and moved from Detroit to Flint, Michigan.

The first Flint Buick, a Marr design, was produced in the summer of 1904. It proved so successful that James Whiting, the wagon works owner, ordered production to begin immediately. By the end of 1904, 37 had been built.

At this point, Whiting had financial difficulties and turned to Flint carriage magnate Billy Durant for assistance. Although reluctant at first, Durant took an extensive Buick test drive and saw the future. In what would prove to be a pivotal event in automotive history, Durant took over Buick.

Once Durant adopted an idea there was no stopping him. He displayed the Buick at the 1905 New York Auto Show and took orders for 1000 before the company had built 40. It was typically Durant: sell them first and then figure out how to build them later.

Durant erected a huge factory in Flint and used the established Durant-Dort carriage dealer network as a ready-made distribution system. His Buick Racing Team, with drivers like Louis Chevrolet, brought wide publicity to the company by winning 500 trophies from 1908 to 1910.

Durant also sold engines and chassis to Sam McLaughlin in Oshawa, Ont., another carriage

entrepreneur, who turned them into McLaughlin-Buicks for the Canadian market.

By 1908 Buick was the biggest auto producer in the United States. In just a few years Billy Durant had gone from being the number one buggy builder to the number one car builder.

In September, 1908, he organized the General Motors Co. with Buick as its anchor nameplate. He quickly brought 30 firms, including Cadillac, Oldsmobile, Oakland (later Pontiac) and AC Spark Plug into his GM holding company.

Durant soon had GM overextended, and was being forced out of the company by the bankers in 1910. Ever the entrepreneur he formed Chevrolet and used it to regain control of GM in 1916, only to lose it for good in 1920.

During those early years of GM, Charles Nash was the corporation's president. Walter Chrysler was general manager of Buick, which continued as a strong nameplate and helped pull GM through a financial crisis in the early '20s.

As Buick continued to build its reputation for reliability and quality, production reached 260,000 cars in 1926. Sold all over the world, including China, Buicks were assembled in—besides Canada—Spain, Belgium, England, Australia and even Java.

Buick survived the Depression and in 1931 introduced its famous overhead-valve, straight-eight engine; in 1936 it brought out the renowned Roadmaster model. This and the other models (the Special, Super, Century and Limited), plus all-steel "turret-top styling" and hydraulic brakes, made '36 a 200,000 vehicle year for the division. It pioneered standard turn signals in 1939, the year after GM's first "dream car," the Buick Y-Job, appeared.

Following military work during World War II, Buick returned to civilian production; sales would reach 550,000 by 1950 and 745,000 by 1955. Its novel torque converter, two-speed Dynaflow automatic transmission came along in 1948, and the compact, high-compression "vertical-valve" V-8 in 1953.

The 1949 Roadmaster Riviera, along with the Cadillac Coupe de Ville and the Oldsmobile 98 Holiday coupe, would bring the "hardtop convertible" to the world in numbers, the same year Buick's famous "portholes" appeared.

In 1954, as a result of a wide range of models, Buick vaulted into third place in North American sales, displacing Plymouth which had been there since 1931. Unfortunately for Buick, some quality problems and a recession caused sales to shrink from almost three-quarters of a million in 1955 to around 250,000 in 1959.

The Special name was moved to a compact car in 1961, fitted with an aluminum V-8. The following year, Buick chopped off two cylinders, made the block out of iron and introduced the first North American production V-6. It was the direct progenitor of the current Buick 3800 V-6.

Like others, Buick suffered through the emissions and fuel economy legislation of the '70s, although it managed to return turbocharging (GM had pioneered it in the early '60s) to the marketplace in 1978. And, as with other GM cars, Buick switched almost universally to front-wheel drive in the 1980s.

To prove the basic soundness of its V-6 engine, Buick ran stock-block V-6s in the famous Indianapolis 500. It won the pole in '85, the first stock-block to do so since 1931. Of the 33 starters in the 1990 Indy, 11 were Buick-powered.

Today, Buick is secure as one of the longest-running industry nameplates. As it celebrated 90 years it proudly billed itself as "the premium American motor car".

BUICK Y-JOB

Although style is a subjective matter that evolves and changes over time, it's generally accepted that the formal emergence of automobile styling took place in 1927. That was the year that General Motors' Cadillac division marked its silver anniversary by introducing a lower-priced "companion" car, the LaSalle, to fill the wide price gap between Cadillac and Buick. A definite decision was taken to apply aesthetic principles to the design of the LaSalle.

Cadillac's president and general manager, Lawrence Fisher, had recently discovered a young man in California by the name of Harley Earl. Earl was working for the Cadillac distributor there creating custom-styled cars for movie

Buick Y-Job.

— GENERAL MOTORS

stars and others. Fisher was so impressed with his talent that he contracted with Earl to come to Detroit to style the new LaSalle. This was really the first time that a manufacturer had applied the aesthetic touch to the automobile in a significant way.

The result of Earl's work was so successful in the new LaSalle that GM president Alfred P. Sloan, Jr., invited Earl to join the corporation to take on the job of creating a new entity called the Art and Colour Section. Reporting directly to Sloan, the section would serve all the car divisions. It was an idea whose time had come because the industry, led by GM, was just evolving the concept of the annual model change.

And who better to define next year's cars than the stylists.

Up to that time car styling had been a branch of engineering, but with the establishment of Art and Colour, GM broke it out as a separate function, later to be called Styling. It would become extremely important to the industry.

Automobile styling flourished in GM, and soon in the rest of the industry. But Earl was not thinking only of next year's models; his fertile, imaginative mind was casting much further into the future. This vision would result in what is generally accepted as the industry's first "dream car": the 1938 Buick Y-Job. It would be another seminal car, just as the LaSalle had been.

This was the era in which the teardrop form, a la the Zeppelin airship, was seen by many as the ideal "streamlined" shape. The Lincoln Zephyr and the Chrysler/DeSoto Airflow models were good automotive examples.

Earl used this idea as his basis, but stepped boldly ahead. With the Y-Job (the letter Y, used to denote experimental airplanes, was adopted for his futuristic car), he in effect extended the concept of the teardrop. In so doing he predicted the shape of the automobile for many years to come.

It was in part to celebrate the coming of age of automobile styling - GM changed the section's name from Art and Colour to Styling in about 1937 - that Harley Earl conceived the Y-Job as a styling exercise. It was his look into the

evolution of the automobile's appearance. The Y-Job, based on a Buick chassis, was the first of what would eventually become a steady stream of "dream cars" from GM and others.

Earl's two-passenger convertible was almost 20 feet (6096 mm) long and had many of the features that would become standard in later cars. Earl dispensed with the running boards, for example, and extended the fenders back into the doors. For a wider appearance, the grille was stretched out horizontally (although with vertical bars) across the front of the car, not placed upright as was the traditional rudimentary cover for the radiator. And the bumpers were wrapped much farther around the fenders than normally.

Earl believed cars were too high, and that lowering them vastly improved their appearance. He achieved some of this effect in the Y-Job by using 13-inch wheels, quite small for the time; the standard Buick's wheels were 15 inches in diameter.

He also felt that the axis of the automobile should be dead level with the ground, not only laterally but longitudinally. This was strongly apparent in the Y-Job, as was another of his ideas, the "power dome" or "helmet" look in the fenders and hood. The Y-Job also had convenience items that would later become standard. It was fitted with electric window lifts, a power operated top, and headlamps concealed behind power operated doors.

GM's Motorama road show extravaganzas were still in the future, so Earl had no ready method of exhibiting his new car except by driving it, which he did. Earl used the Y-Job as his personal transportation for several years, impressing his country club friends.

During World War II, automobile styling languished, and production even stopped between 1942 and '45. The Y-Job went into storage until 1947; it went on to serve as inspiration for cars into the '50s. By this time, however, Earl's mind was again jumping ahead with such visions as tail fins, wraparound windshields and acres of chrome.

The 1938 Buick Y-Job was a significant vehicle. It pointed the way for American automobile styling and established the concept car idea as a method of probing the future, testing public reaction to new directions, and even on occasion leading public taste. For this it has earned a permanent place in automotive history.

33

CADILLAC'S EARLY ENGINEERING ACHIEVEMENT

Cadillac established its motto "The Standard of the World" based on its outstanding engineering leadership. Although it started humbly enough in 1902 with a small one-cylinder engine, it quickly developed a reputation for excellent workmanship and leading edge technology.

Cadillac's roots and early reputation can be traced back to a no-nonsense New Englander by the name of Henry Martyn Leland. Leland was born in Vermont in 1843, didn't graduate from high school, and soon found himself working for the Springfield Arsenal. A lack of education didn't hold Henry back as he quickly displayed a genius for things mechanical. His next job was

1905 Cadillac.

– BILL VANCE

with Colt Firearms.

Close, consistent tolerances were critical in making firearms, and Leland soon developed a passion for precision and the interchangeable parts that it made possible. This made him so valuable to his next employer, Browne and Sharpe Manufacturing Co., a Providence, Rhode Island toolmaker, that he was soon their travelling salesman and technical expert. His territory included Detroit.

Sensing the growing importance of Detroit as an industrial city, he and two partners set up a toolmaking company in 1890 called Leland, Faulconer and Norton, soon to be Leland and Faulconer when Norton departed. Their products included gears, marine engines and grey iron

34

castings, the latter being of such precision that customers were willing to pay a premium for them.

Leland and Faulconer was soon supplying engines to Ransom Olds for his Curved Dash Oldsmobiles. Also at about the same time a group of Detroit businessmen financed a company called the Detroit Automobile Co., with Henry Ford as its chief engineer.

When Ford seemed more interested in building racing cars than passenger cars, the backers set out to wind up the business in 1902. They called in Henry Leland to appraise the equipment, but as they became familiar with him, asked if he would work with them in a new venture. Leland and Faulconer would supply the engines and drivetrains, and their new company, which they called the Cadillac Automobile Co., after Detroit's founder, would build the bodies and assemble the cars.

Two cars were sold in 1902, their first year, but early in 1903 when they showed the Cadillac at the New York Auto Show, orders were received for 2300. Cadillac then had to figure out how to build them, a problem it seemed unable to resolve, with the result that they were always behind in orders. Recognizing the need for better management, Leland and Faulconer were invited to merge with Cadillac, which they did. The result was the reorganized Cadillac Motor Co., formed in 1905 with Henry Leland as general manager.

With the production problem solved, Cadillacs quickly built up a reputation for quality. Cadillac added a four cylinder engine for 1905. Then in 1907 Leland began using the Swedish high precision Johansson gauge blocks to maintain the close tolerances he demanded. With these, Cadillac was able to boast that some 250 of its parts could meet a tolerance limit of 1/1000th of an inch.

This would soon be demonstrated in a dramatic fashion. To prove that Cadillac's parts were fully interchangeable the English Cadillac distributor, Fred Bennett, entered three of them in the Royal Automobile Club's parts standardization trial. All manufacturers were invited, but only Cadillac took up the challenge.

Three new Cadillacs were chosen at random and driven to the Brooklands track. Under the scrutiny of R.A.C officials, the cars were completely disassembled, the parts scrambled, some new ones substituted, and the cars reassembled. They were then driven 500 miles (805 km) around the track without failure.

It was an impressive feat in an era when most cars were still largely hand assembled, each one a little different from the next. It laid the foundation for the rapid development of the industry, and won Cadillac the coveted Dewar Challenge Trophy.

In 1908 William Durant, a carriage making magnate from Flint, Michigan, organized a holding company called General Motors. He already controlled Buick, and quickly began building his empire, adding Oldsmobile, and then bringing in Cadillac in 1909. Although Durant would lose control in 1910, Cadillac under Leland and his son Wilfred would continue to prosper.

Then, in about 1910, an event took place that would result in one of the most significant events in automotive history. Byron Carter, a good friend of Henry Leland, was killed as the result of a cranking accident while trying to start a car. Leland had had his engineers working on trying to eliminate the difficult and dangerous crank starting, and Carter's death made him redouble these efforts.

Leland was also acquainted with a brilliant young engineer named Charles Kettering who had just developed an electric cash register for the National Cash Register Company in Akron, Ohio. Leland asked him if he could help with the invention of an electric starter. Kettering reasoned that the same principle he had used for the cash register might work for a starter. This was that an electric motor could be temporarily overloaded without damage.

In trying to solve the starter problem, previous inventors had worked on the basis of continuous operation. It was Kettering's genius to recognize that this was an unnecessary requirement. He applied the same logic to the gasoline engine starter that he had to his electrified cash register and it worked. Cadillac introduced the electric starter and the condenser ignition system to the world on its 1912 model. The starter did double duty; once the engine was running the starter changed to a generator and charged the battery. The introduction of the electric starter won Cadillac an unprecedented second Dewar Trophy.

Cadillac's reputation was now soundly established as an engineering leader. It would go on to other accomplishments. In 1915 it discontinued the four cylinder engine and switched exclusively to V-8s. It was not the world's first user of V-8s, but Cadillac, along with Ford's first V-8 in 1932, would go a long way toward popularizing this type of engine.

Although not as dramatic as its interchangeable parts and electric starter, Cadillac would continue to consolidate its reputation for engineering prowess. It introduced 4-wheel brakes in 1923, Duco quick-drying paint in 1924, crankcase ventilation in 1925, formal automobile styling in the 1927 La Salle, and the synchromesh transmission in 1928. In 1930 Cadillac startled the world with its new V-16 engine, which marked the beginning of its bid to become the supreme American luxury car. It was followed less than a year later by a spin-off V-12, giving Cadillac buyers a choice of eight, 12 or 16 cylinders.

Times have changed and competition has intensified, but in its heyday Cadillac's engineering leadership earned it the legitimate title of Standard of the World.

CADILLAC 1949

Nineteen-forty-nine was an important year for our domestic auto industry. After three years of building warmed-over versions of pre-World War II cars, GM, Ford and Chrysler were anxious to offer something new. After all, some of the smaller companies such as Studebaker and Hudson had been able to bring out their new models more quickly.

Of the Big Three, only Cadillac had beat the 1949 watershed by a year, introducing its new post-war model in 1948. Oldsmobile managed to bring its new car out in 1948-1/2. But while the '48 Cadillac, with its tail fins inspired by the Lockheed Lightning P-38 twin-engined fighter plane, started a new craze in auto styling, the big news would

1949 Cadillac.

—BILL VANCE

come in 1949.

In addition to complete new models from the Big Three, Cadillac, along with Oldsmobile, introduced a new type of powerplant that would become dominant in North American cars for the next quarter century. This was the high-compression, short-stroke, overhead valve V-8.

Henry Ford had demonstrated back in 1932 that the smoothness of V-8 power could be brought into the popular priced field. And while Cadillac and others had used V-type engines for many years, it was the introduction of the 1949 Cadillac and Oldsmobile high-compression V-8s that really set the trend.

The potential of high compression was no

37

and V-16s (the world's first in 1930).

It's no surprise, then, that Cadillac would again be an engine innovator. Oldsmobile's V-8 was similar in design to Cadillac's, although smaller. The 1949 Cadillac V-8 had oversquare dimensions with a bore and stroke of 3.8125 x 3.625 inches (96.8 x 92.1 mm), which yielded 331 cubic inches (5.4 litres) of displacement. Its 7.5:1 compression ratio helped it to develop 160 horsepower.

With the top horsepower rating among current domestic cars, it's not surprising that the Cadillac's performance was sparkling. Car tester Tom McCahill of *Mechanix Illustrated* magazine tested a Cadillac sedan, along with an Oldsmobile and a Buick, in the February, 1949, issue and said that the Cadillac was "… unquestionably America's finest automobile to date."

Of the Cadillac's performance, Tom in his usual fashion couldn't simply say that it was fast, or had quick acceleration. It had, said Tom, the "… acceleration and flash of the finest imported racing cars. And it climbs hills like a gazelle."

Translated into numbers, Tom reported that this flashing gazelle would sprint from zero to 60 mph (96 km/h) in 12.1 seconds, a very good time for that era. He estimated the top speed at more than 105 mph (168 km/h).

In styling, Cadillac, along with Oldsmobile and Buick, pioneered in 1949 what would become a very popular model, the hardtop

secret to engineers. Walter Chrysler had used higher than normal compression ratios to advantage back in the 1920s, and his cars developed a reputation for spirited performance. But the limiting factor on compression ratios was the quality of gasoline available.

Although the addition of tetraethyl lead to gasoline, starting in the 1920s, had improved its anti-knock qualities, it took the forced development of higher octane aviation fuel during WW II to bring about better anti-knock qualities in normal motor gasoline. General Motors' research chief, the brilliant Charles Kettering, played an important role in both the development of leaded gasoline, and in the high compression engines that could take advantage of it.

For Cadillac, the introduction of a new type of powerplant was not surprising. Cadillac had a proud tradition of engineering innovation dating back to the early part of the century.

In 1908 it had won the Royal Automobile Club's coveted Dewar Trophy for the use of interchangeable parts. Cadillac repeated the feat in 1912 when it pioneered the electric starter, along with electric ignition and lights, inventions that Kettering is credited with, and which really liberated the automobile for use by many more people, particularly women.

Late in 1914 Cadillac moved straight from an in-line four-cylinder engine to a V-8, and during the 1930s, offered not only a V-8, but also V-12s convertible. It would, according to the acerbic McCahill, convert only to a hardtop. The idea was to make a hardtop car look like a convertible, so two-door coupe models were given pillarless side designs, and (usually) two-tone paint jobs to suggest that the top would really retract.

Cadillac offered the feature in the series 62 Coupe de Ville, Buick in the Roadmaster Riviera (the first use of the Riviera name by Buick), and Oldsmobile in its 98 Holiday Coupe.

But in spite of the tail fins, and the advent of the hardtop convertible, the engine was really Cadillac's big 1949 news. It was light yet powerful, weighing 188 pounds (86 kg) less than the 345 cubic inch (5.6 litre) side-valve V-8 it replaced. It also proved to be a popular competition engine, being used in many applications such as drag racing, and in such road-racing cars as the Cadillac Allard. It helped Cadillac win *Motor Trend* magazine's very first Car of the Year Award, chosen by none other than John Bond who would go on to become owner/editor/publisher of rival *Road & Track*.

The horsepower remained at 160 for three years, and then in 1951 Chrysler brought out its famous Firepower Hemi V-8, which developed 180 horsepower out of the same 331 cubic inch (5.4 litre) displacement that was used by Cadillac. It didn't take Cadillac engineers long to scurry back to their drawing boards and come up with a new four-barrel carburetor, dual exhausts and bigger valves, and 190 horsepower for 1952. Chrysler countered with 195 in 1954, and thus began the famous, or infamous, depending upon your point of view, horsepower race of the '50s and '60s. The 1949 Cadillac 62 series convertible was surely the original post-World War II "American Dream Machine."

CADILLAC V-16

1939 Cadillac V-16.

— BILL VANCE

It is one of the ironies of automotive history that some of the largest and most luxurious cars ever built were offered for sale during the worst of economic times. Cadillac is a good example.

The reverberations from the October, 1929, stock market crash that led to the Great Depression of the '30s, had hardly settled when Cadillac introduced the mightiest car it had ever offered: the exclusive V-16. On Jan. 4, 1930, Cadillac stunned the world and put arch-rival Packard in the shade when it introduced its 16-cylinder model 452 at the New York Automobile Show.

It was powered by a 452 (from whence it derived its name) cubic inch (7.4 litre) overhead valve engine with the banks set at a very narrow 45-degree angle. Hydraulic valve silencers were used and each bank of cylinders had its own fuel and exhaust system, making it in effect like two 8-cylinder engines attached at the crankcase. It developed 165 horsepower and was said to be capable of propelling the heavy (close to 6000 pounds, or 2722 kg) vehicle at speeds up to 100 mph (161 km/h).

In addition to the luxurious V-16 engine, buyers of the 452 could choose from an extensive selection of coachwork. According to Walter McCall's definitive work, *Eighty Years of Cadillac LaSalle*, 54 semi-custom Fleetwood body styles, ranging from "sporty roadsters, convertibles and coupes to big sedans, phaetons and stiffly formal

40

"limousines and open-front town cars," could be fitted to the V-16's 148-inch (3759 mm) wheel-base chassis.

Considering the economic times, it is somewhat surprising that Cadillac was able to find customers for 2887 of these opulent cars in 1930. In 1931, Cadillac brought out a companion V-12 model (its regular model, which it continued to build, had been a V-8 since 1915) and this, plus the increasing bite of the Depression, no doubt contributed to the V-16's 1931 sales plummet to only 364. In spite of annual sales counted in the hundreds and occasionally even in the dozens, Cadillac hung on to the V-16 engine through the '30s.

The overhead valve V-16 was kept through model year 1937, and then for 1938 was replaced with a side-valve V-16 with a very wide 135-degree angle between the cylinder banks. In fact, it was so flat that it almost appeared to be a horizontally opposed layout. But it was 13 inches (330 mm) lower, and this meant that the firewall could be extended over the engine to provide more interior vehicle space.

With 431 cubic inches (7.1 litres), it displaced slightly less than the earlier V-16 but produced about the same 185 horsepower developed by the more recent of the narrow-angle engines. Although the change from overhead to side valves may be viewed as a retrograde step, the new V-16 was definitely pointing the way to the future in one respect with its equal 3-1/4-inch (82.5 mm) "square" bore and stroke dimensions. But it was strictly utilitarian in appearance; the beautiful aesthetics of the ohv V-16 engine were gone.

The 1930s saw the demise of such Cadillac competitors as Franklin, Marmon, Peerless and Duesenberg, but the resources of General Motors allowed it to carry the V-16 right through model year 1940, when it was quietly discontinued.

I recently had an opportunity to inspect and drive a 1939 Cadillac V-16 seven-passenger formal sedan that has historical links with *The Toronto Star*. Its first owner was none other than Joseph E. Atkinson, the astute publisher/philanthropist who took over *The Star* in 1899 at the age of 23 when it was a feeble publication with a circulation of 7000. By the time Atkinson died in 1948, it had grown into Canada's largest newspaper with a circulation of 345,000.

Atkinson kept the Cadillac and, after the settlement of his estate, it passed into the hands of a Mr. Ardagh Scythes who was in the "slicker" raincoat business. In approximately 1957 Graham Neilson, scion of the Neilson chocolate family, bought the Cadillac and, as he recalled recently, "did a fair amount of touring in it." He also remembers that it got seven miles per gallon in the city and nine on the highway.

Recently the car came into the hands of its fourth owner, Al Webster of Al Webster Classic Cars in Gormley, Ont. Al deals in classic cars of all kinds, but he also feels they should be exercised. "I like to drive my cars," he says, "not just let them sit around and look at them." His regular "beater" car, as he calls it, is a lovely '41 Cadillac convertible.

Driving the V-16 is an experience not soon forgotten, but I would be less than candid if I told you that it drives anything like the cars of today. The steering is heavy and ponderous with a huge bus-like steering wheel, and keeping a steady course requires constant attention. The brakes take fairly high pedal pressure, but the car does ride quite well.

The engine, however, runs with turbine-like smoothness and easily took us up to 60 mph (96 km/h), with much more on tap. Neilson stated that the V-16 will pull away from rest in high gear, a feat we didn't try out of respect for Mr. Webster's clutch. And we forget that three-speed transmissions back then had no synchromesh on first gear.

The car is finished in beautiful gleaming black, and is immaculately detailed thanks to some extra TLC by Al's son, Bruce. It still has the original Cadillac motor rugs with Atkinson's initials on them, and the two pillows and wedge-shaped foot rests which match the upholstery.

In spite of the irony of their birth, it's a grand thing that such vehicles have been preserved. Without them, it would be difficult to imagine, given the downsized, compact and mini-cars of today, what these huge land yachts of the classic era were really like.

CHEVROLET CORVETTE 1953

By the early 1950s North America was becoming aware of the sports car, a vehicle meant for fun rather than work. It wasn't to be practical, or to be particularly comfortable. Its purpose in life was to give driving pleasure, to make the trip more exciting than the arrival.

The quintessential sports car in those days was the English MG, first in the TC model with its high wire wheels and rakishly cut fenders, and then in the TD, which had been "Americanized" with smaller, less appealing disc wheels and more softly sculpted lines.

The stunning Jaguar XK120 roadster, also from England, introduced as a 1949 model really

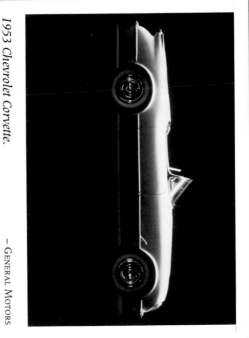

1953 *Chevrolet Corvette.*

gave sports car interest a boost with its outstanding performance and beautifully flowing style.

American automakers were not immune to infection by the sports car bug. Several of the smaller manufacturers such as Crosley, Nash and Kaiser-Frazer marketed two-seater sports roadsters. Willys-Overland had even brought out a jaunty sports version of that famous World War II workhorse, the Jeep, and called it a Jeepster.

At this time General Motors also started to take an interest in the sporty car phenomenon, having noted in particular the great popularity and sheer beauty of the Jaguar XK120. To test the waters, GM styling chief Harley Earl designed, and had GM staff construct, a long, low Buick

"Dream Car." He named it the LeSabre and began showing it around the country in 1950. Although the LeSabre, and a sister car, the Buick XP-300, were ridiculed by the wind-in-the-face sports car set, the general response indicated to Earl that there was a genuine interest in an American sports car. By late 1951 he was sure of it and set about to get General Motors into the market.

Earl established a small secret studio with a few trusted sports car enthusiast designers and they went to work. In order to keep costs down, the design was based on Chevrolet components, but it was to be a long way from a Chevy sedan, both in concept and appearance.

The centre of gravity was lowered to 18 inches (457 mm) above the ground, and the engine was set three inches (76 mm) lower and seven inches (178 mm) further back than in the sedan. At 102 inches (2591 mm), the wheelbase was also 13 inches (330 mm) shorter.

By the spring of 1952 the chassis had been developed. Then a full-size clay model of the car was built from which a very realistic plaster mock-up was fashioned. Harley Earl knew that recently appointed Chevrolet chief engineer Ed Cole was a dyed-in-the-wool car enthusiast, so Earl chose Cole as one of the first Chevrolet Division officials to view the "car."

Cole was ecstatic; observers of the scene say that he literally jumped up and down with excitement. Cole's enthusiasm helped the division gain corporate approval to display the Corvette, as it was subsequently named, as a dream car at GM's annual Motorama show.

The Corvette's public introduction came at the Motorama held in New York's Waldorf Astoria hotel in January, 1953. Audience response was extremely positive and it was decided almost immediately to produce 300 Corvettes for sale. Interest was running so high that Chevrolet officials felt the public wouldn't wait until 1954 for their American sports car. The goal was to start building Corvettes by June, 1953, a mere five months away; it was an incredibly short time in which to produce a new model.

To meet this deadline would require unorthodox methods; there simply wasn't time to produce the traditional metal dyes required to stamp out steel body panels. It was decided to make the car bodies out of glass-reinforced plastic (GRP), which later became known generically as fiberglass. GRP development had been accelerated during World War II as a possible replacement for scarce steel in some applications, and after the war it was being used for building boats. Some small specialty car manufacturers, and even Kaiser-Frazer, used it for car bodies. General Motors was familiar with the material, having constructed many of its show cars out of glass fibre.

The Molded Fiber Glass Body Co. of Ashtabula, Ohio, was the successful bidder for the Corvette body parts, and through a prodigious effort during those hectic few months, managed to supply them to Chevrolet's equally frenetic Flint, Mich., plant in time. The first official production Corvette rolled off the line on June 30, 1953 - within deadline!

The initial 300 Corvettes, all of them Polo White, were designated as 1953 models. Production of '54s continued in Flint until December, 1953, when the operation was moved to St. Louis, Mo., the exclusive home of Corvette production for 30 years. They have been built in Bowling Green, Ken., since 1984.

Buyers of the first Corvettes found their performance spirited, if not up to the level of the Jaguar. Cole's engineers had increased the power of the Chevrolet 235 cubic inch (3.8 litre) "Blue Flame" six from 115 to 150 horsepower by such accepted hot rodding techniques as raising the compression ratio and fitting a higher lift camshaft. The sedan's single downdraft carburetor was replaced by three side-drafts for two reasons: better breathing, and the very practical one that the original wouldn't fit under the Corvette's sleek hood. The radiator header tank was also moved to the side of the engine for hood clearance.

The biggest disappointment from the enthusiast's point of view was the "Powerglide" two-speed automatic transmission: no manual was offered, a situation that Chevrolet didn't rectify until the 1956 model. In spite of this, performance was reasonably brisk. *Road & Track*

magazine's June, 1954, road test of the Corvette recorded a zero to 60 mph (96 km/h) time of 11 seconds, and a top speed of 106 mph (170 km/h).

This was only one second and 16 mph (26 km/h) slower than the vaunted Jaguar XK120. It's a far cry from today's performance, but it was more than respectable for the era. Although the Corvette was almost discontinued in the mid-1950s because of slow sales, the appearance of the two-seater Ford Thunderbird sportster in 1955 convinced GM to stay in the sports car market. Countless thousands of Corvette enthusiasts are thankful for that decision.

CHEVROLET 1955

1955 Chevrolet Bel Air Convertible.

— BILL VANCE

The 1955 Chevrolet was one of the most popular Chevrolet models ever made, a truly significant milestone in the history of America's most prolific automotive nameplate. It achieved this recognition for two very good reasons: styling and performance.

By the early 1950s the bloom was in danger of going off the auto industry. The car-starved condition caused by the interruption in auto production during World War II, plus the pent-up demand of war workers and returning armed service personnel, had been satisfied. Competition was heating up, and Chevrolet knew it would need attractive new models to maintain its traditional sales superiority over arch-rival Ford.

Chevrolet's products had begun to look a little stodgy by the early '50s. The revived Ford Motor Company's strong styling statement with its full pontoon-bodied 1949 models, along with its reputation for performance built around the V-8 engine, made it a formidable competitor. A vigorous response was obviously required from Chevrolet.

In June, 1952, GM corporate approval was given to the Chevrolet Division to go ahead with a brand new model for 1955. And it really was to be all new. In addition to a complete restyling, it was also to offer a V-8 engine, not a first for Chevrolet because they had had one in 1917-18, but certainly a modern breakthrough. Chevy had, after all, become strongly identified with six-cylinders, having been powered exclusively by an overhead valve "Stovebolt Six" since 1929.

So while the stylists worked on a more attractive skin for the Chevrolet, chief engineer Ed Cole and his staff got busy designing a new powerplant.

Cole was no stranger to V-type engines. He had started working for Cadillac in 1940 where the only engines were V-types, and had been that division's chief engineer when it brought out the sensational 1949 short-stroke, overhead valve V-8. That, along with the famous Oldsmobile Rocket 88 engine, set the post-war American V-8 powerplant design trend.

The new Chevy V-8 had the latest advancements in engine engineering. It had a five-bearing, forged steel crankshaft, oversquare bore and stroke (3.75 by 3.00 inches; 95 by 76 mm), "slipper" type aluminum pistons, and ball-stud valve rockers. The use of thin wall castings yielded an engine that, at 535 pounds (243 kg), was 35 to 40 pounds (16 to 18 kg) lighter than the Chevrolet six, and 50 pounds (23 kg) lighter than competitor Ford's 272 cubic inch (4.5 litre) V-8.

All of this styling and engineering alchemy came together in the 1955 Chevrolet, introduced in the fall of 1954. It was electrifying. The "Motoramic" styling was clearly meant to give buyers the impression they were getting a car that was very similar to its much more expensive stablemates in the General Motors lineup.

With eyebrows over the headlamps, and a vertical pillar wraparound windshield, it strongly resembled its top-of-the-line corporate sibling Cadillac. Its forward canted eggcrate grille, reminiscent of the one on the expensive Italian Ferrari, gave it an exotic aura, and the belt line dip just aft of the front door was a nice styling touch that seemed to accentuate lowness.

Chevrolet stylists had reached that touchstone of excellence in American styling; they had made the car look longer, lower and wider all at once, although its dimensions weren't much different from the 1954 model. It had the same 115-inch (2921 mm) wheelbase as the previous year's car, and was actually almost an inch shorter in overall length, although it was a few inches lower thanks to a flatter roof profile.

The new Chevrolet wasn't just show; thanks to its new Cole-inspired optional V-8 (the six continued), it also had plenty of go. With 162 horsepower out of its 265 cubic inch (4.3 litre) displacement, it was potent enough. But if that wasn't sufficient, there was a "Power Pack" available with a four-barrel carburetor and dual exhausts that pumped it up to 180 horsepower.

As recently as 1951 Chrysler had scooped the industry with its 180-horsepower, 331 cubic inch (5.4 litre) "Fire Power" hemispherical combustion chamber V-8. Now, just four years later, the low priced Chevrolet was producing the same power out of a much smaller, lighter engine.

Road & Track magazine tested a 180-horse-power, overdrive-equipped '55 Chevy in its Feb. '55 issue, and recorded a 0-to-60 mph (0-to-96 km/h) time of 9.7 seconds, a very quick figure for the day. Top speed was 104.7 mph (169 km/h), achieved in direct drive third gear; it was actually a couple of mph slower in overdrive.

Tom McCahill, *Mechanix Illustrated* magazine's road test guru, probably summed it up best when he said the new V-8 changed Chevrolet's image from a somewhat stodgy performer into a "truly sensational wildcat."

Chevrolet was a hot one in the showrooms too. The 1955 model sales total was 1.64 million units compared with 1.15 million for the 1954 model. And the Chevy V-8 "small block" engine proved to be one of the most successful power-plants of all time, so successful that it is still a GM stalwart 40 years later.

The 1955 Chevrolet was an American classic of its era, and that's the reason old car buffs now regard it, and the derivative '56 and '57 models, as among the most desirable collector cars of the '50s.

CHEVROLET CAMEO CARRIER

Pickup trucks can be pretty luxurious today, available as they are with almost all of the amenities of cars. This has contributed to their extreme popularity; they are now often used just as passenger vehicles, with little or no cargo-hauling applications.

But it wasn't always so. Pickups were originally developed as no-nonsense working vehicles, and that's what they remained for many years.

In the early days of trucking, pickups were mostly spinoffs of passenger cars. Manufacturers simply cut off a car body behind the front doors, closed in the rear of the cab and attached a utility box to the frame. This was largely their

1958 Chevrolet Cameo Carrier.

— BILL VANCE

form during the 1920s and '30s.

Then during the 1940s, particularly after World War II, light trucks began to take on a persona of their own. They evolved as larger, sturdier purpose-built commercial cargo haulers rather than extensions of the automobile line. They had all of the mechanical necessities, but little thought was given to luxury or style. Trucks were still primarily designed as the basic transportation tool of farmers, tradesmen and businesses.

That image began to change in the 1950s. And if one vehicle could be identified as the watershed in this movement, the harbinger of the more glamorous pickup, it would be the

49

1955 Chevrolet Cameo Carrier. There was also a companion GMC model called the Suburban, which differed only in trim and engine options.

Nineteen-fifty-five was a big year for Chevrolet in both cars and trucks. The division's car was completely restyled into what was called the Motoramic Chevrolet. With its new wrap-around windshield, egg-crate grille, "eyebrow" headlamps and high taillights, the '55 Chev exhibited strong Cadillac traits.

To go with this stunning style, buyers could opt for the division's new 265 cubic inch (4.3 litre) short-stroke, overhead valve V-8 engine. With the 180 horsepower "Power Pack" option (162 hp was standard), it was a real tiger, quite a change from the image of the staid "stovebolt" Chevy six.

The year's second series of Chevrolet trucks (the first units were carryover '54s) that appeared in March, 1955, were strongly influenced by the Chevrolet car. These "Task Force" trucks, as they were called, also received wraparound wind-shields, egg-crate grilles and eyebrow lamps. A 36 percent increase in glass area provided greatly improved visibility. The new V-8 was available in trucks too.

With its standard pickups starting to take on a little style, Chevy decided to go all out with a really dressed up model called the Cameo Carrier. Using the Deluxe cab with its wraparound rear window as a base, designers applied more stylish interior and exterior appointments and paint treatment.

The most striking difference was the use of fibreglass panels on the sides and rear of the standard cargo box. These brought the sides of the box out flush with the cab. At the rear, a panel dropped down below the tailgate to reveal the spare tire.

Cameos got a special two-tone paint job in Commercial Red and Bombay Ivory accents. This, and the use of such additional dress-up items as full chromed wheel covers and grille, made the Cameo look like no pickup that had gone before.

Unfortunately, this style didn't come cheap; this dude truck carried a price approximately 25 percent above the regular pickup. Since trucks were still seen basically as utility vehicles, few buyers were willing to pay the premium, and only 5220 Cameos were sold in its short first model year. Sales sputtered even more in 1956 when just 1452 found buyers.

For 1957 Chevrolet gave the Cameo a new grille and different paint schemes and managed to coax sales up to 2244. Nineteen-fifty-eight would prove to be the Cameo's last year. Despite quad headlamps and yet another revised grille, Chevy sold only 1405 units. The Cameo was replaced in mid-year by the Fleetside pickup, which carried many of its predecessor's styling cues without the premium price.

While the Cameo Carrier didn't sell well

conveyances for passenger transportation. It set the trend for glamorous pickups, and as such, deserves its little place in history.

enough to justify continuing it, it is interesting that at the same time as it was about to disappear, Ford would enter the luxury truck market with its stylish car-like 1957 Ranchero. Based on the chassis of their station wagon, Ford stylists fashioned a vehicle that was half car and half truck; the forward part including the front seat was just like a car, but there the similarity ended. The body lines carried back unbroken and had a cargo box where the back seat and trunk would be. It started a new class of luxury truck, and it would take Chevrolet until 1959 to respond with its El Camino.

The Cameo Carrier could be credited with prompting a similar effort from the Chrysler Corp. When Chrysler saw the Cameo, it wanted to get into the glamor truck business too, but couldn't afford to spend much money. Its approach was to remove the rear fenders and bumper assembly from a custom cab half-ton Dodge pickup and replace them with the rear fenders of a '57 Dodge two-door Suburban station wagon. The result was the 1957 Dodge Sweptside 100 pickup. Dodge dressed it up with whitewall tires, chrome wheel covers and a two-tone paint job, and made it the most stylish Dodge pickup ever.

Although the Cameo Carrier had not been a commercial success for Chevrolet, it did demonstrate that trucks no longer needed to be dull and frumpy workhorses, but could also be stylish

Chevrolet Corvair

1965 Chevrolet Corvair.

— Bill Vance

The most unusual car and arguably the most technically interesting one to come out of Detroit in the 1960s was the Chevrolet Corvair. At a time when the domestic industry staple was a large, front-engined, rear-drive sedan with a solid rear axle, usually powered by a cast iron V-8 engine, Chevrolet's general manager, Edward Cole, later a General Motors president, took a daringly innovative approach with the Corvair.

Its engine was an aluminum, horizontally opposed (flat), air-cooled six-cylinder located in the rear of the car. Unit construction was used for the body/chassis, and suspension was independent all around utilizing coil springs.

It's no coincidence that these features sound amazingly similar to a certain German economy car because it *was* the Volkswagen that inspired the Corvair; the Corvair was in fact to be an "American Volkswagen." During the late 1950s the American auto manufacturers, particularly the Big Three, GM, Ford and Chrysler, had become increasingly alarmed about the rising penetration of small foreign cars into the North American market. They also noted the strong sales of the 100-inch wheelbase American Motors Rambler American.

The most popular of the imports was the German Volkswagen, and Ed Cole was convinced that he could build a bigger and better Volkswagen. Thus, although the Corvair had the

52

same general layout as the Volkswagen, the Corvair's wheelbase was 108 inches (2743 mm) compared with the VW's 94.5 (2400), and at 2450 pounds (1112 kg), it weighed 800 pounds (364 kg) more than the German economy car. And while the Volkswagen had a 36 horsepower 72.7 cubic inch (1.2 litre) four cylinder engine, the first Corvair was powered by an 80 hp, 140 cubic inch (2.3 litre) six.

The Big Three answered this small-car challenge with models they called compacts, and introduced them in late 1959 as 1960 models. Ford and Chrysler chose a conventional route for their import fighter; the Ford Falcon and Chrysler (soon to be Plymouth) Valiant had water-cooled, six-cylinder engines mounted in the front of the car driving the rear wheels. Neither had independent rear suspension. General Motors, on the other hand, through its Chevrolet division, unabashedly copied the Volkswagen's layout.

The Chevrolet Corvair, in spite of its technical novelty, or perhaps because of it, didn't sell as well as its main rival, the Ford Falcon. Buyers of domestic economy cars apparently weren't as ready as those who bought imports to stray off the well trod technological path. The Corvair did, however, appeal to the sporty car set, and when Chevrolet introduced the Corvair Monza version in mid-1960, it sent its new compact off in a whole new market direction.

The Monza was nothing more than a Corvair Deluxe 700 coupe fitted with such items as bucket seats, special wheel covers, chrome rocker moldings and vinyl upholstery. But these seemingly minor styling changes were enough to alter the Corvair's personality and turn it into a much more desirable model. The Monza stood apart from mundane workaday Corvairs, and sales took off.

Chevrolet knew it was on to something, and set out to really exploit the sporty car segment. For 1961 it introduced a four-speed manual transmission, and then for 1962 it became even more exotic with the debut of the Corvair Monza Spyder. It came in coupe or convertible form, and its most outstanding feature was an exhaust-driven supercharger, known as a turbocharger.

A turbocharger is an air pump that pushes more air into the engine than it would breathe normally. And more air and fuel in means more power out. It is driven by a gas turbine installed in the engine's exhaust stream, and since it is activated by waste gas, it supplies what can be considered "free" horsepower. Chevrolet, therefore, along with Oldsmobile, which had introduced its turbocharged F-85 Jetfire model just a month earlier, made General Motors the world's first manufacturer to offer turbocharging on production cars.

In 1965 the Corvair underwent a big change. Not only did it get a beautiful all-new longer, lower and wider body, it also got a significantly improved rear suspension system in which the swing axles were replaced by a fully articulated suspension much like the Corvette's. This corrected a major design criticism of the Corvair.

The Monza was relegated to a mid-pack model and the Corsa became the top of the line Corvair. The turbocharger was now an option on the Corsa and horsepower was listed as 180, up from 150, from the same 164 cubic inches (2.7 litres).

Along with the new styling and better suspension for 1965 came something else: a nasty surprise in the form of a book entitled *Unsafe At Any Speed*. In it a Washington, D.C., consumer advocate lawyer by the name of Ralph Nader savaged the auto industry with the allegation that it was building unsafe cars. He singled out the Corvair for a particularly scathing attack, saying, among other things, that its swing-axle suspension (as used on the '60 to '64 models, although the '64 did get a lateral leaf spring "camber compensator") caused the rear wheels to "tuck under." Nader alleged that this caused the Corvair to flip over during even relatively low-speed cornering.

This book, plus stiff competition from Ford's sporty new Mustang introduced in 1964, sent Corvair sales into rapid decline; it would ultimately be discontinued in 1969. The turbo-charger option continued to be offered until 1966, before it was eliminated.

Turbos would disappear from automobiles for about a decade because it was simply easier and cheaper to get more power by building a bigger engine. In spite of the failure of the Corvair in the marketplace, not all justified, and not all related to its technical novelty, Chevrolet and sister GM Division Oldsmobile had paved the way for turbocharging, even though circumstances weren't quite ready for it. Corvairs, particularly turbocharged models, are now sought after collectibles.

CHRYSLER–DESOTO AIRFLOW

While the Chrysler/DeSoto Airflow models that came out of the Chrysler Corp. in 1934 are most remembered for their unorthodox styling, they were also interesting cars from an engineering perspective. They brought together several emerging trends. These related to streamlining, as the science of aerodynamics was then called, and such engineering features as the forward-mounted engine/chassis layout with its "between-the-axles" seating. Also, its body was made almost exclusively of steel at a time when other manufacturers still used a considerable amount of wood.

The Airflow's styling was based on the "Art Deco" school of design, the clean, pure lines that

1934 DeSoto Airflow.

— CHRYSLER CANADA

took over from the elaborate and sinuous "Art Nouveau". Art Deco was a significant and influential art form between the two world wars.

Although overshadowed by its styling, the Airflow's forward-mounted engine and between-the-axles seating could be called the real beginning of the current "cab-forward" design.

The genesis of the Airflow idea, according to lore, occurred in 1927 when Chrysler research chief Carl Breer was driving home from work one day and became entranced by the ease and freedom with which a flock of birds flew gracefully through the air. The "birds" proved instead to be military aircraft on manoeuvres. Why not, he thought, apply the same stream-

55

lining principles to the motor car. He wasn't the first person to have this thought; Gabriel Voisin and Edmund Rumpler, among others, had pursued the same idea in Europe.

Breer proposed his idea for a "rational" engineer's car to Walter Chrysler. Chrysler agreed, and Breer and his two brilliant associates, Owen Skelton and Fred Zeder, Chrysler's crack "Three Musketeers" engineering team, began work on their new concept.

They consulted aviation pioneer Orville Wright, and engaged an aerodynamicist named William Earnshaw to do some wind tunnel testing. One of the surprising findings was that some cars of that era were more aerodynamically efficient going backwards than they were forward!

At that time, the teardrop was considered the ideal streamlined shape. This meant that a vehicle had a long, sloping profile, and to achieve this, Breer had to move the seating forward on the chassis to provide sufficient headroom under the sloping roof of the body.

The result was that the engine had to be relocated some 18 inches (457 millimetres) ahead, above the front axle line rather than behind it. The outcome was not only increased passenger space, but a reversing of the vehicle's usual 45/55 percent front/rear weight distribution. This gave the car a much better ride by cradling the passengers between the axles, and by reducing

the pitching motion when road irregularities were encountered. It also gave the car better directional stability.

Thus, in the pursuit of a solution to a styling problem, the engineers made important technical advancements. The forward-mounted engine and between-the-axles seating soon became the industry standard.

A prototype Airflow was ready by late 1932, and Walter Chrysler was impressed enough to give his approval for production. The target was 1934 - to celebrate the 10th anniversary of the corporation, and, apparently, because it was rumored that General Motors was also preparing a streamlined design. This rushed development would, unfortunately, sow the seeds of the Airflow's later failure.

In addition to the forward engine and seating, Breer and company designed a body/chassis that was much stronger than normal. Although not true unit construction, it was made almost entirely of steel, and by tying the body and frame members tightly together and using a steel framed superstructure, they gave it some of the strength of unitized construction. To demonstrate the ruggedness of the Airflow, Chrysler personnel pushed one off a 110-foot (33 metre) cliff in Pennsylvania, and then drove away in the battered but still drivable car. It was an impressive stunt.

The new Chrysler/DeSoto was introduced as

planned at the New York Auto Show in January, 1934. Truly a break with the past, the car reflected the Art Deco styling theme then in full bloom. Its Zeppelin-inspired body had a vertical bar "waterfall" grille, and lines that curved up gently from the triple-bar bumper, and continued over and back to swoop down to a tapered tail.

The Airflow met with mixed but generally favorable reaction. Orders came in, but due to the hurried development and the radical new design, Chrysler wasn't able to get the car into production until April, 1934. The result was that only about 12,000 Chrysler and 14,000 DeSoto Airflows were sold in 1934, and much of the public's ardor had cooled.

Chrysler facelifted the 1935 Airflows under the guidance of famed industrial designer Norman Bel Geddes. As a hedge, however, the company also revamped its conventional Airstream model at the same time.

When 1936 sales slipped to just 6274 Chrysler and 5000 DeSoto Airflows, the decision came to discontinue the car after the 1937 model year. The Airflow experience would settle Chrysler into a conservative styling mode that would characterize its products for almost 20 years.

The usual reason cited for the Airflow passing from the scene was that its styling was just too far ahead of its time. This was true in part, but there was also the fact that it never fully recovered from its rushed development.

The Chrysler/DeSoto Airflows, despite their failure in the marketplace, did initiate the between-the-axles seating layout which would become virtually universal in cars. For this, as well as its Art Deco lines, it deserves its niche in automotive history.

CHRYSLER 300S

1955 Chrysler C300.

– CHRYSLER CANADA

Let's jump back four decades, over today's front-drive aero cars, over muscle cars, over pony cars, over the original Big Three compacts, right into the middle of the 1950s when gasoline was cheap and the flashier and sportier a car looked, the better it was considered to be.

World War II was now a distant memory and the economy was healthy. City families were flocking to the suburbs for their little patch of green, and motor manufacturers recognized that, along with the suburban home, a car was a powerful image-builder. And they were more than eager to provide the flashy cars that projected one's persona and reflected those optimistic times. Station wagons and sports cars

were particularly potent image enhancers.

When it was clear that the sports car movement was strong, spawned by such marques as the MG and Jaguar from England, Chevrolet countered the imports with the Corvette in 1953. Ford followed with the Thunderbird in 1955. Chrysler also played its part, but in a slightly different way than General Motors or Ford.

Chrysler sorely needed a status car. Under the presidency of K.T. Keller who had taken over from Walter P. Chrysler, the company's styling had grown dull and stodgy. Keller had always insisted that a man should be able to easily enter and drive a Chrysler product while wearing a hat. Thus its cars had rooflines that were higher than the competition's making them look tall and stubby.

When Keller became chairman in 1950 and a new president by the name of Lester (Tex) Colbert took over, the stage was set for change. Colbert's new models, with styling led by Virgil Exner who had been with Studebaker during the development of their advanced 1947 models, came out for 1955. They had a much more contemporary "Forward Look," and Colbert wanted something special, a kind of "halo car," to draw attention to them.

Then as now, Chrysler was smaller and less wealthy than GM and Ford, and it couldn't afford to bring out an all-new model. But it did want something sporty, so it resorted to the next best trick in the car builder's shell game: it raided the parts bin.

The cupboard turned out to be far from bare. In the engine department there was the great hemispherical combustion chamber V-8, by now nicknamed the Hemi, that could provide boulder-moving power. It had been introduced in 1951 and had outstanding development potential beyond the original 180 horsepower.

The New Yorker, smallest of the corporations's large sedans, contributed the two-door body. To give the new car some distinctiveness the New Yorker body was fitted with rear quarter moldings from the Chrysler Windsor. The Chrysler Imperial provided the two-piece grille.

To provide better handling, the engineers

pulled out a few of the tricks, such as a stiffer suspension, they had learned while competing in the Mexican Road Race, a free-for-all "stock car" race run up the spine of Mexico in the early 1950s.

An image car requires good performance, so the Hemi was hopped up with two 4-barrel carburetors, a hotter cam and solid valve lifters to a heady 300 horsepower, the highest available at that time. The only transmission fitted was Chrysler's new two-speed "PowerFlite" automatic. The interior of the car was dressed up with leather and an Imperial instrument panel, including an impressive 150 mph speedometer.

With clever mixing of these easily available corporate components, Chrysler had, therefore, developed the 1955 C300 super car. It fulfilled its intended role admirably. It gave Chrysler a sporty image and enough performance to bring a look of chagrin to many a Corvette owner's face. And it didn't cost the corporation the bank.

The 300s soon became the scourge of the stock car circuits, a great selling tool in an era when "Win on Sunday, sell on Monday" was more than just a catchy slogan. At the National Association for Stock Car Auto Racing speed week held on the sands of Daytona Beach, Florida, in February 1955, a C300 romped to a win in the stock production class with a two way average of 127.58 mph (205 km/h) on the hard packed sand. It beat out runner-up Cadillac by more than seven mph (11 km/h), and in so doing won the Tom McCahill trophy. McCahill, *Mechanix Illustrated* magazines's famed car tester, was trials director that year.

Chrysler knew that spectators and racing enthusiasts might not necessarily buy a 300. But the company also knew that the public loved to bask in the reflected glory of a winner; buyers were convinced they were getting the same sterling engineering qualities, and a little of the cachet, in their workaday Plymouths and Dodges.

For 1956 Chrysler raised the displacement to 354 cubic inches (5.8 litres) and changed the name to the 300B. The top horsepower available - with a 10.0:1 compression ratio - was 355, which pushed the V-8 over the then magic one hp per cubic inch, an achievement that Chevrolet would tout as an American "first" the following year. Chrysler then marched annually up the alphabet to the 300L of 1965 (they missed I), earning them the name "letter cars." In those early years the 300s became steadily more powerful - 375 hp in 1957, 380 in 1958.

Nineteen-fifty-eight was the last year for the 300 Hemi (although it would be revived six years later as the Dodge "Hemicharger"), and by the early '60s the 300 had started to lose some of the hard edge that had distinguished the early ones.

Like so many others, Chrysler gradually depreciated the value of a grand nameplate by fitting it to more prosaic vehicles. And by the mid-60s manufacturers were starting to install their largest engines in smaller models to create the so-called muscle cars, and the 300 no longer held performance superiority. What could perhaps be referred to as the original "muscle car," the Chrysler 300 had been defanged.

The 1965 300L was the last of the letter-cars. The plain 300 continued on until 1971, but the magic was gone. The name was revived by Chrysler in 1979 but was short-lived; as the saying goes: "you can't go home again." Times had changed. A new era of front-drive, fuel-efficient cars was dawning, and the time of the big, ground-pounding, pavement-ripping V-8s of the 1950s and '60s had passed.

CHRYSLER K-CARS

If Walter P. Chrysler was looking down from auto mogul heaven, he must have been proud of Lee Iacocca during the latter's heyday. In fighting for the Chrysler Corp. from 1979 to 1982 and finally rescuing it, Iacocca displayed the same drive and spirit that Walter P. had shown 60 years earlier when he saved Willys-Overland. Chrysler then rejuvenated Maxwell Motors Corp. and proceeded to turn it into the Chrysler Corp. in 1925.

But a man can't do it all alone; he needs hardware. And just as Chrysler had the "Good Maxwell" to help him with the transition, Lee Iacocca had his corporation's front-wheel drive K-car.

1981 Dodge Aries.

— CHRYSLER CORP.

Badged as the Dodge Aries and Plymouth Reliant, no product in modern automotive history would be so extensively previewed and have so much riding on its angular shoulders. The K-car's mission was no less a task than to save the Chrysler Corp.

U.S. automakers had been caught in the gyrations of the turbulent 1970s. The decade saw oil crises in 1973-74 and '79, tightening fuel economy and emission requirements, increasing foreign competition, and a marketplace that seesawed between demanding small and large cars.

Chrysler's initial response to small-car demand in the '70s was to rebadge Japanese Mitsubishi products and market them with names like

Dodge Colt and Plymouth Champ. This gave the company time to produce its own cross-engine, front-wheel drive clone of the Volkswagen Rabbit (now Golf). The subcompact Dodge Omni/Plymouth Horizon twins were launched as '78 models.

But Chrysler also foresaw the need for larger, but still economical cars, a prediction vindicated by the '79 energy crisis. As the Omni/Horizon design neared completion in 1976, Chrysler began work on its new fwd car, code-named the K-car. Although the design was well advanced when Iacocca joined Chrysler in 1978, and he had no part in it conception, he would wholeheartedly embrace it.

While the Omni/Horizon helped Chrysler, the company still lost U.S. $1.1 billion in 1979, the biggest business loss in U.S. history. The media had a field day, making such comments as "looking into the abyss," and "teetering on the brink of bankruptcy." It would take a special person to rescue Chrysler.

Fortunately such a man became available when Henry Ford II fired Iacocca after 32 years with the Ford Motor Co. Invited to join Chrysler, Iacocca came on his own terms; he would start as president and soon be made chairman. He was 55, and as he noted in his biography: "At this point in my life, I had no interest in working for somebody else."

In seeking the government loan guarantees required to save Chrysler, Iacocca and his new management team, many of whom were from Ford, had a silver bullet: the K-car. And to persuade the U.S. Congress to approve the guarantees, he had to reveal Chrysler's future product plans. Thus, the K-car was so widely exposed in the year prior to introduction that its official debut as a 1981 model was almost anticlimactic.

What Iacocca showed was a squared-up sedan, coupe and station wagon whose angular outlines yielded an unimpressive coefficient of drag of 0.45 to 0.51, despite a reported 320 hours in the wind tunnel.

The K-car had a 99.6 inch (2530 mm) wheelbase and was 175 inches (4445 mm) long overall. This was 5.3 inches (135 mm) less wheelbase and six inches (152 mm) less length than the 1980 GM X-cars (Chevrolet Citation, Pontiac Phoenix, et al.) but the box-like shape gave it virtually the same interior space. Chrysler called it a six-passenger, but in truth the K-car was more comfortable for five.

Power came from a Chrysler-made, transversely mounted 2.2 litre four-cylinder engine (the company's first four since 1932). The overhead cam, 84 horsepower engine drove the front wheels through a standard four-speed manual or optional three-speed automatic transaxle. A Mitsubishi Silent Shaft 2.6 litre four was optional.

The unit-construction K-car had MacPherson struts in front and a beam axle at the rear and weighed just over 2400 pounds (1089 kg). Despite its rather appliance-like approach to life, the Aries/Reliant proved to have a heart of gold.

Chrysler survived, thanks to the sale of some 410,000 1981 K-cars, compared with 195,000 of the rear-wheel drive Dodge Aspen/Plymouth Volares that it replaced. By 1983 Chrysler was out of the woods financially, and Iacocca was proudly able to pay off U.S.$833 million in guaranteed loans.

Chrysler would go on to spin off many K-car derivatives, so many in fact that it became almost an industry joke. But the company would have the last laugh. Its minivans - Dodge Caravan and Plymouth Voyager - also had K-car components and would scoop the U.S. auto industry, establishing a lead in vans that Chrysler still holds.

The original K-car is gone now, replaced in 1989 by the Dodge Spirit/Plymouth Acclaim, although many of its components carry on. And Iacocca is gone from Chrysler, retiring in 1992 and turning the reins over to a younger team. But he established his name as a company rescuer alongside such titans as Alfred P. Sloan, Jr., who did the same for General Motors, and Walter P. Chrysler himself. The humble K-car has its place in history too for its contribution to saving a venerable corporation.

CONTINENTAL
Mark II 1956-57

1956 Continental Mark II.

– BILL VANCE

The Continental Mark II introduced by the Ford Motor Co. as a 1956 model had two missions: to recapture the magic of the original pre-war Continental, and to displace Cadillac from its position as North America's most sought after luxury car.

The original Continental came to life in the late 1930s when Ford Motor Co. president Edsel Ford (the first Henry's son) asked the company's chief stylist Eugene Gregory to develop a sporty car for his personal use. Gregory used the V-12-powered Lincoln Zephyr, which had been introduced in 1936 as a junior Lincoln, as the base for Edsel's special.

The result was so popular with the country

club set that Ford decided to put it into production as the 1940 Lincoln Continental, which eventually became identified as the Mark I. This original Continental was built from 1940 to '42, and again following World War II from 1946 to '48.

Ford had planned to replace the Mark I when it went out of production in 1948, but the company was short of money so its resources were concentrated on developing new post-war designs for established lines such as the Ford and Mercury. The '49 Ford was a stunning success, and was followed by another complete redesign in 1952, which enabled Ford to recover second place in the industry behind GM, moving the Chrysler Corp. back to third.

64

With its return to prosperity, Ford could set out to recapture the original Continental's glamor. The goal was straightforward: to create the most luxurious American car on the market. Although it would not necessarily be the largest or most powerful car available it was to be the epitome of elegance, a reincarnation of the great classics of the 1930s ranking with the world's top models such as the Rolls-Royce.

The projected selling price was to be in the $7500 to $8000 range (it would ultimately be $10,000), about twice as much as regular Lincolns and a tremendous price for a car in those days. Even at that it was not seen as a money maker for the company; Ford was more intent on knocking Cadillac out of its vaunted position as the domestic industry's most prestigious nameplate.

To accomplish this task a group known as Special Products Operations was established. This would later become the Special Products Division, and in 1955, the Continental Division as Ford strove to emphasize the importance of this new model by giving it division status.

Following consideration of several styling competition proposals, the same method that had been used for the '49 Ford, Ford's executive committee selected one put forward by the Special Products Division's own team, which included Gordon Beuhrig of Cord 810/812 fame. The style chosen was termed "modern formal,"

and it combined clean, modern lines with enough styling cues to relate it to the original Continental.

The Mark II had an understated eggcrate grille, and the long-hood/short-rear-deck motif of the original was retained. Horizontal fender lines swept back to a point just ahead of the rear wheels, where they took a slight kick-up and continued to the tail lights.

A rear blind spot caused by the formal roof line also harked back to the original Continental, but the real link was the "Continental" spare tire shape that was molded into the trunk lid. The spare tire was mounted beneath this hump in the rear of the trunk, preserving some authenticity, but making trunk loading an awkward operation.

In an era characterized by garishness, chrome trim was used sparingly and no two-tone paint jobs were available. The fuel filler cap was concealed behind the left tail light, a direct take-off on Cadillac.

Extensive preparation and care went into finishing the body. Panels were painted and hand-sanded several times before the final two coats of lacquer were applied. Chrome plating was used extensively, not for appearance, but for protection on such places as the end panels of the doors and on the door jambs.

Although there was a certain cost-no-object approach to the Mark II, the line was drawn at the powertrain. A V-12 was considered, but quickly dismissed as too expensive. For 1956 Lincoln was introducing a new 368 cubic inch (6.0 litre), V-8 and this was chosen to power the Mark II, but fitted with special cast aluminum valve covers. Each engine would be dynamometer tested. The rest of the driveline, including the standard equipment three-speed automatic transmission, was also from Lincoln, although more assembly and testing time would be lavished on the Mark II's powertrain than on regular Lincolns. Air conditioning was the only option.

In addition to being understated on the outside, the Continental was also quietly elegant inside. When leather upholstery was ordered, for example, it was from Bridge of Weir in Scotland. The brushed-finish instrument panel held four round dials of equal size, and even included a tachometer.

The Continental Mark II came in only one body style, a hardtop coupe. Although a convertible was theoretically offered, only one or two were apparently ever built. Consideration was also given to using a retractable hardtop but this was abandoned; the idea would see brief production as the 1957-59 Ford Skyliner.

After considerable advance publicity, introduction of the Mark II took place at the 1955 Paris Auto Show. This was followed by several exclusive "by invitation only" private showings back in North America.

In spite of its price, about 1300 Continentals were sold during the last quarter of 1955, many of them to celebrities such as politician Barry Goldwater, actor Frank Sinatra, and the Shah of Iran. But after this initial sales surge it was all downhill for the Continental Mark II. Only about another 1300 were built during 1956, and 450 in 1957, when production ceased.

There are probably several reasons for the early demise of the Mark II. First was the $10,000 price, which although high, is still said to have lost Ford $1000 on each car. Another reason could have been its plain appearance in an era of styling flamboyance. And with its body-on-frame construction, it was becoming technically obsolete compared with the regular Lincoln line, which was switching to unit construction for 1958.

In spite of its lack of market success, the Continental Mark II stands as a beautiful example of marrying classic elegance with modern engineering. It was a valiant attempt to recapture the spirit of the great cars of the thirties, but unfortunately for Ford, that era was gone forever.

CORD

1937 812 Cord.

– BILL VANCE

The Cord car was built by Errett Lobban Cord's Auburn Automobile Co. of Auburn, Ind., from only 1929 to 1936, and with a hiatus at that. But it made a mark on automotive history out of all proportion to its short production life. While the cars had some advanced engineering features such as front-wheel drive, they are probably remembered as much for their style as they are for their technical novelty.

Cord cars were unusual, and so was the man who built them. E.L. Cord was born in 1894 in Warrensburg, Mo., just about the same time as the North American automobile was beginning to evolve. A few months earlier, Charles and Frank Duryea of Springfield, Mass., had constructed and driven what is generally recognized as America's first practical gasoline-powered motor car.

And in 1893 a futuristic Toronto patent attorney by the name of Frederick Featherstonhaugh had commissioned John Dixon's carriage works, and William Still, an electrical engineer, to build an electric car for his personal use. It was Toronto's first automobile.

The industry soon flourished, and the ambitious and flamboyant young Cord along with it. By the early 1920s, he was selling Moon cars so successfully in Chicago that his annual income was the then enormous sum of $30,000.

67

He wanted more in life, however, and with the opportunity for a principal position, left Moon to join the troubled Auburn Automobile Co., which had an unsold inventory of some 500 cars in its storage lot.

Being the natural salesman that he was, Cord realized that sizzle was required along with the steak. Cord had the cars repainted in bright, appealing colors and quickly sold the whole batch.

His initial success in moving the Auburn inventory earned Cord control of the company, which he was soon able to turn around. He then began to assemble an empire by acquiring the Duesenberg Motor Co. of Indianapolis, a maker of large luxury cars.

Not surprisingly, Cord wanted to produce a car bearing his own name and capitalize on the huge price gap between the moderate Auburn and the expensive Duesenberg. The resulting model, called the Cord L-29, appeared in 1929. It was a stunning vehicle.

To keep its contours low, Cord stipulated that the L-29 have front-wheel drive. He engaged engineer Carl Van Ranst to design it. Van Ranst had worked with the famed Harry Miller in building the front-drive Miller racers that were dominating the Indianapolis 500. Van Ranst used a solid, de-Dion-type front axle, and mounted the drum brakes inboard.

The L-29 became the first American front-driver to go into serious production. The sleek silhouette, fitted with bodies from several coach builders such as Murphy and Hayes, was complemented by the long hood necessary to house the straight-eight engine and drive-train. The stylish vehicle won several awards, including the 1930 Monaco Concours d'Elegance, and was favored by many Hollywood celebrities.

Despite the onset of the Depression in 1929-30, Cord's empire did reasonably well for a while, but by the early '30s times were getting harder. Slow sales caused the L-29 to be dis-continued in December, 1931.

The Cord Corp., which in addition to Auburn and Duesenberg had expanded to include Lycoming Engine Co., Columbia Axle Co., Checker Cab Manufacturing, and Century Airlines, badly needed a new car model to enhance its image.

Following months of rumors, E.L. announced in January, 1934, that Cord would produce a new car "of radically advanced design, engineering and performance." It was to be a "baby" Duesenberg.

Cord finally set his engineers and stylist Gordon Buehrig to work on the new car early in 1935, and they had a prototype built by August. E.L. was delighted with it. He decided that it would be a Cord not a Duesenberg, and ordered that production models be ready for the 1935 fall motor shows, a mere 15 weeks away.

It was an extremely short deadline, but the dedicated staff almost literally "banged together" the cars, as one exhausted worker termed it. Although the American Automobile Manufactures Association rules stipulated that at least 100 cars must be built to qualify for display as a production model, E.L. blithely ignored the rule. The actual number of cars ready was estimated to be as low as 11.

The Cord 810, as it was called, was a sensation on the show circuit. Buehrig had produced a stunningly styled body that incorporated all of the best contemporary features and some new ones, treading where no other stylist had dared go. The 810 was not bound by any styling heritage, and it showed.

The long alligator hood was a simple, unadorned yet elegant shape that somewhat resembled a coffin, earning the Cord its "coffin nose" nickname. The grille was comprised of seven horizontal bars running completely around the front end from door to door. It was simple but effective.

In the voluptuously rounded pontoon fenders lurked hidden pop-up headlamps. The door hinges were concealed, there were no running boards, and the interior featured a stepdown design. An aerodynamic fastback rear end finished off the car.

The Cord carried some unusual engineering features. The Lycoming side-valve, 289 cubic inch (4.7 litre) V-8's 125 horsepower was sent to the front wheels through a four-speed pre-selector transmission located ahead of the engine. Unit construction was used from the cowl back, and the car rode on a generous 125-inch (3175 mm) wheelbase.

The Cord 810 was hailed by the public, and although buyers were promised cars by Christmas, it was April, 1936, before restive customers began getting them.

And when they did hit the road, some weaknesses of the rushed development showed up. There were engine overheating problems, and the transmission often didn't stay in gear. This, plus a high price, resulted in the sale of only 1174 1936 Cords.

Supercharging was an option for the 1937 812 Cord, which raised horsepower to a reputed 170. Despite the addition of two new models, only 1146 of the '37s found buyers. Production ceased at that time, and the body dies were used to build Hupmobiles and then Grahams.

E.L. Cord, who went on to other endeavors, died in 1974, but his memory lives on in the beautiful cars he produced. They have a cherished place in history, and are valuable collectibles today.

CROSLEY HOTSHOT/SUPER SPORTS

With the current revival of interest in small, open sports cars brought about by the very successful Mazda Miata, many car buffs are looking back fondly and comparing it to British sports cars of the '50s and '60s. It's particularly similar to the original Lotus Elan of 1962 to '74.

During that era the British had pretty well defined the genre. Such cars as the MG, Triumph, Austin-Healey, and Jaguar were regarded as quintessential sports cars.

Sports car lovers felt that domestic manufacturers were not really capable of or interested in producing a real sports car. The opinion appeared to be confirmed when the first Chevrolet Corvette arrived in 1953 with a two-speed automatic Power-glide transmission; no manual gearbox would be available until 1956.

But the Corvette was not our first post-World War II production sports car. The honor of building it fell to Powel Crosley, Jr., of Cincinnati, Ohio.

Crosley got into the automobile business in the very early years, building his first car, a six-cylinder model called the Marathon, in 1909. It was not successful, but he tried again in 1913 with a cycle-car called the DeCross. After this failure, Crosley gave up and went to work for other auto manufacturers.

It wasn't long before the adventurous Crosley discovered a new thing called radio, and began building them commercially. By the early '20s,

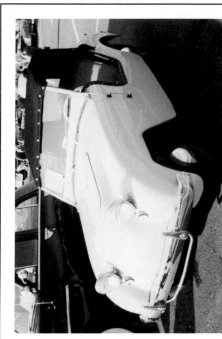

1949 Crosley Hotshot.

– BILL VANCE

his Crosley Corp. had become the world's largest radio manufacturer. To give his customers something to listen to he also established his own radio station, WLW in Cincinnati.

He soon branched out into other home appliances, and his Crosley "Shelvadoor" refrigerator was the first to have shelves in the doors. An avid baseball fan, he was the owner of the Cincinnati Reds, who, naturally, played their home games in Crosley Field.

But his interest in a basic, economical automobile had never died. Now with his financial success he was able to afford another try at entering the business. In 1939 he started building a tiny car powered by a two-cylinder, air-cooled, 39 cubic inch (0.6 litre) engine made by the Waukesha Motor Co. of Waukesha, Wisc. This sold in modest numbers, but was built for only three years before Crosley and other automakers suspended car production to go into war work.

Auto production resumed in 1945, and in those car-starved years Crosley prospered moderately with his diminutive cars, now much improved with four-cylinder engines. In order to give his model line some lustre, he brought out a sports car, the Crosley Hotshot, in mid-1949.

The Hotshot resembled an inverted bathtub, and at 145 inches (3683 mm) in length, it wasn't much bigger either. The tiny roadster was a pretty spartan car. It had no doors and no trunk lid, the engine was covered by a flat metal hatch, the spare

tire was bolted onto the rear deck, and the windshield was a flat piece of glass. The headlamps perched up on the hood like a bug's eyes.

The Hotshot's wheelbase was only 85 inches (2159 mm) and it had tiny 4.50 by 12 inch tires. Power went to the rear wheels through a three-speed, floor-shift transmission. And the Hotshot was a real flyweight at just over 1100 pounds (499 kg).

It was under the simple hood that was to be found the Hotshot's best feature: its overhead cam, five-main-bearing, four-cylinder engine. Although it displaced only 44 cubic inches (725 cc) it produced 26.5 horsepower at 5400 rpm, an almost unheard of speed for an American production engine.

Before most other manufacturers had discovered the advantages of oversquare engine design - greater bore dimension than stroke - Crosley had showed the way with a 2.50 inch bore and a 2.25 inch stroke (63.5 mm x 57.1 mm). And overhead cams had rarely been seen in American production cars.

The Hotshot soon gained a reputation of sorts by winning the first six-hour endurance race for sports cars held in Sebring, Florida in 1950. With a mere 725 cc of engine displacement it could hardly be expected to out-run the Jaguars, Ferraris, Aston Martins and Cadillac-Allards that were entered, and of course it didn't.

What it did do, however, thanks to its tiny

engine, was win what was called the Index of Performance, a formula based on distance travelled and engine size. With such small displacement the little Crosley had to just cruise around at 52 mph (84 km/h) to finish first, which it did.

Tom McCahill, *Mechanix Illustrated* magazine's car tester, put one through its paces for his eager readers. He reported in the Oct. 1949 issue that it achieved a zero to 60 mph (96 km/h) acceleration time of 28.1 seconds, and reached a top speed of 74 mph (119 km/h).

To place this in the context of the times, he reported that the MG TD took 22.8 seconds to reach 60 (96), and topped out at about 80 mph (129 km/h). But McCahill also noted that the MG had a 1.25 litre (76 cubic inch) engine, and that it cost almost twice as much as the Hotshot.

The Crosley was even tested in the biggest sports car event of them all, the 24 hours of LeMans in France. A modified Hotshot was entered in the 1951 race and was doing very well - hitting up to 95 mph (153 km/h) on the straights - until its generator burned out.

McCahill admitted that the Hotshot, and the Super Sports that followed it - its main difference was that it had doors, and a very high 10.0:1 compression ratio - had many shortcomings. They were simply and crudely built, but this at least contributed to a price of less than $1000. McCahill's conclusion was that it was a "tin tub on wheels with a fine engine," and he summed it up as "dollar for dollar and pound for pound... one of the greatest sports cars ever built."

Alas, even the quick, economical little sports car couldn't save Crosley Motors. There were now lots of new cars around for people to buy. From 29,089 Crosleys sold in 1948, its best year, sales declined annually until by 1952 demand fell so low that the company was forced to stop building cars.

Powel Crosley had made a valiant attempt to bring a small, economical car to the North American market. And his Hotshot/Super Sports was a sports car truly built for having fun. Unfortunately it was just too small, and was also ahead of its time, so it remains a tiny chapter in automotive history.

CUNNINGHAM

B.S. Cunningham Co.

The Cunningham name has been prominent on the American automobile scene in two different eras. The first was the James Cunningham, Son and Company of Rochester, N.Y., which built large, high-quality cars from 1907 to 1936.

The other Cunningham car builder, although smaller and shorter lived, was much more interesting. It was the B.S. Cunningham Co. of West Palm Beach, Florida, set up by American millionaire Briggs Swift Cunningham in 1950.

Briggs Cunningham was to the manor born. His father had inherited considerable wealth, some of which he had used to help found a new company by the name of Procter and Gamble.

Cunningham C-4R Roadster.

– Bill Vance

His mother fell heir to a large inheritance from railroad and utilities holdings in Cincinnati,

Ohio. Cunningham was born in Cincinnati in 1907, the same year, interestingly enough, that Tom McCahill came into the world in Larchmont, N.Y. McCahill would grow up to become *Mechanix Illustrated* magazine's famed car tester, and a close friend of Cunningham's.

Cunningham attended prep school and ended up at Yale University, also McCahill's alma mater, where he planned to become an automotive engineer. He lasted only a year or two there, however, and left to pursue what seemed to have been a rather carefree existence of activities like golf and sailing. He married and

73

took his new wife on a honeymoon to Europe where he bought an Alfa Romeo and a Mercedes-Benz.

Upon his return to the United States, Cunningham became interested in car racing and, with the help of some friends, constructed a hybrid racer using Buick Century and Mercedes-Benz parts. It was called the Bumerc and it raced in the New York World's Fair Grand Prix in 1940, unfortunately crashing into a lamp post.

After World War II Cunningham became acquainted with a couple of Long Island stock car racers by the name of Bill Frick and Phil Walters. They ran a garage called Frick-Tappett Motors (Walters raced under the pseudonym Ted Tappett) and along with other project cars, had created the Fordillac, a 1949 Ford powered by a Cadillac engine. The Fordillac immediately caught Cunningham's attention, and he wanted to race one in the famous 24-hour endurance race held every year at Le Mans, France.

Le Mans was the world's most renowned auto race where victory brings a great sense of national pride for the winning country. Although American cars had made respectable showings there - a Stutz finished as high as second in 1928, with Chryslers coming third and fourth - an American car had never won Le Mans.

The Fordillac looked like a winner, but the Le Mans officials wouldn't allow him to enter it because of its hybrid nature. With the Fordillac ineligible, Cunningham entered two Cadillacs in the 1950 race, one an ugly, square, box-shaped car that was immediately dubbed "Le Monstre" by the French. They ended up 10th and 11th, a quite remarkable showing for what were definitely not racing cars. This convinced Cunningham that he could construct an American car that could be victorious at Le Mans. He purchased Frick-Tappett Motors and moved the whole operation to West Palm Beach where it became the B.S. Cunningham Co.

The first prototype racing sports Cunningham was called the C-1, but it would be C-2 that they would use to contest Le Mans. His cars were an amalgam of parts from various cars, but at its heart was the all-new 331 cubic inch (5.4 litre) Chrysler "Hemi" overhead valve V-8 engine that developed 180 horsepower in stock form. By raising the compression ratio (McCahill said they did this by using Cadillac pistons!) and fitting four carburetors, output was easily raised to 220 hp. A Ford front suspension was used, Cadillac brakes were fitted, and the steering came from Chrysler. It was all clothed in somewhat bulbous, but not unattractive, roadster bodywork finished in white with two blue stripes down the middle.

By a herculean effort, three C-2s were readied for the 1951 LeMans race in just three months. There was no time for testing and they were sent to the ship with hardly any miles on them. Two spun out of the race, but the third ran in second place for six hours before it suffered burned valves and bearing problems due to the inferior quality of the gasoline provided. It finished in 18th place, not auspicious, but at least it had proved that it could run right up with the best.

In order to qualify as an automobile manufacturer and be eligible to run at Le Mans, Cunningham had to build at least 25 cars, so the C-3 was developed for road use. It came in coupe and convertible models with styling and bodies by Vignale of Italy.

His team was back at Le Mans in 1952 with the C-4R model, which was six inches (152 mm) narrower, 16 inches (406 mm) shorter, and several hundred pounds lighter than the 3400-pound (1543 kg) C-2. Again, two of the three cars failed when the Hemis, now up to 235 horsepower, had valve troubles. But the third, shared by Briggs himself, finished fourth after he made an iron-man drive of 18 hours.

Cunningham brought his racers back to Le Mans in 1953 where they placed third, seventh and 10th, and in 1954 when they finished third and fifth. A new car with an Offenhauser engine competed unsuccessfully in 1955, the last year that Cunningham would try to win Le Mans in an American car. An American victory would have to wait for the mighty Ford GT40s of the '60s.

It had been a valiant attempt by a privateer, even a very wealthy one, to win Le Mans for America. But Briggs Cunningham had given it

his best with American components, which at that time were not quite up to the levels of such European competitors as Jaguar and Ferrari.

Although Briggs Cunningham was unsuccessful in winning the world's top sports car race in an American-built car, he did win international acclaim for his country in another of his loves - yacht racing. In 1958 he piloted the twelve metre racing yacht, *Columbia*, to victory in the America's Cup Challenge.

DeLorean
The Man and His Car

1983 DeLorean.

– Richard Spiegelman

It's not easy to start a car company. The most successful in modern North America, Kaiser-Frazer Corp., lasted only 10 years, in spite of being launched in the car-starved 1940s. Preston Tucker's try in the same era was defeated after he built just 51 of his radical rear-engined cars.

Malcolm Bricklin attempted in the 1970s in New Brunswick, and even with the infusion of $23 million (Cdn) of taxpayers' money, only produced some 2850 of his sporty gull-wing, fibreglass two-seaters. The only man to launch a successful and lasting high volume car company in the last 50 years was Soichiro Honda of Japan.

Another who tried was John Zackary DeLorean, and he had the right credentials. While none of the above entrepreneurs was a trained professional engineer, DeLorean was, and a very good one. He had a strong technical/business background, and was tall (six-foot-four; 1930 mm), handsome and charismatic.

Born in 1925 in a Detroit working class neighbourhood, DeLorean studied hard and gained an engineering scholarship to Detroit's Lawrence Institute of Technology. After graduation he joined Chrysler in its co-op engineering program, obtaining a master's degree in automotive engineering. Finding Chrysler too big, he soon moved to Packard and was head of research and development in just four years.

When Packard and Studebaker merged in

76

1954 DeLorean could see their future dimming. He thus moved to the Pontiac Division of GM as a staff engineer in Sept. 1956. His rise through GM was meteoric. He became chief engineer, then general manager at Pontiac in 1961, and helped transform its staid image with such cars as the GTO and Grand Prix.

DeLorean was promoted to general manager of troubled flagship division Chevrolet. Its administration was a mess and it was losing market share. By 1972 he had it turned around, and soon found himself on GM's fabled Fourteenth Floor as group executive of the Car and Truck Group. This placed him, at the age of only 47, in the running for the GM presidency.

But DeLorean found executive row dull and suffocating, far from the excitement of running a car division. Perhaps because of this his maverick personality began to emerge. He eschewed corporate blue, and black oxfords, in favour of sharp Italian suits and fancy boots. He let his hair grow, divorced, and dated models and movie stars. He thought some of GM's practices were ethically questionable, and tried to encourage the hiring and promotion of minorities.

John DeLorean was out of step with GM, and this led to resignation from his $650,000 job in April 1973. Rumor had it that he would have been fired had he not resigned; it was clear that neither party was happy.

When DeLorean left GM he became almost a

folk hero. Here was a brilliant, socially conscious engineer leaving the world's largest corporation, ostensibly due to stifling internal politics and disagreement with many of its bottom line driven practises which he saw as ignoring customer interests. It was seen as a sacrifice few men would make for their personal ethics.

In late 1975 DeLorean announced that he was going to build his own "ethical car." He had an uncanny ability to attract top talent to his fledgling DeLorean Motor Co. Bill Collins, who had overseen the downsizing of GM's full size 1977 cars, was recruited as chief engineer. C.R. (Dick) Brown, organizer of Mazda's dealer net-work, was hired to do the same for DeLorean. Famed Italian Giorgio Guigiaro would style the DeLorean.

Some financing was raised by selling dealerships for $25,000 each. Entertainer Johnny Carson and a Canadian banker named Edmund King also invested a million dollars. DeLorean reportedly used almost none of his own money.

While development of the car went on, DeLorean began courting vulnerable governments to provide a plant. By the summer of 1978 he had a verbal agreement with the government of Puerto Rico. Unknown to them, however, he was also negotiating with the British for a plant in Belfast, Northern Ireland, and with the Republic of Ireland for one in Limerick. When he began to play one off against the other, Puerto Rico and Ireland withdrew.

Britain, anxious to create employment and reduce sectarian violence in Northern Ireland, agreed to finance a plant in the Dunmurray district of Belfast.

In the meantime Lotus Cars of England had been engaged to help develop the car. Friction soon developed between chief engineer Collins and Colin Chapman of Lotus because Collins saw Lotus as lacking commitment. Collins soon departed, and the car that emerged drew heavily on existing Lotus designs.

The DeLorean car turned out to have a rear-engine layout with a centre backbone frame forked at each end. The front "Y" contained the radiator, steering, suspension and fuel tank. The rear one held the transmission and a Peugeot-Renault-Volvo all-aluminum, 2.8 litre V-6 mounted behind the rear axle, a highly unorthodox placement for a modern car.

Body material for the low, crisply styled two-seater coupe was fibreglass, externally clad with stainless steel. Its other distinguishing feature was the use of gullwing doors, à la the 1950s Mercedes-Benz 300SL coupe.

The first car rolled out in January 1981. DeLorean's charisma was still strong, and when American car publications were allowed to test a DeLorean they dearly wanted to like it. In spite of this, Car and Driver magazine said it had "...a tendency to get very antsy at hyper speeds over bad pavement. Hopping, darting and corkscrewing motions are not the stuff of confidence."

Road & Track reported that "the rear-engine layout tends to produce a pendulum effect...resulting in the back end getting loose and out of shape." And all testers complained of its poor visibility and a claustrophobic interior.

While the car met lukewarm acceptance from the press, DeLorean was attempting to get more and more money out of the British government. There were hints of scandal, and questions in Parliament before they finally called a halt at $250 million (U.S.). With support gone the company went into receivership in Feb. 1982 after 7500 cars had been built.

The final chapter in this rags-to-riches tale came when John DeLorean was arrested by the FBI in Los Angles in Oct. 1982. He was charged with cocaine dealing, presumably to help finance his failed company. He was later acquitted on the defence that the government agents had used entrapment.

It was a tragic and ironic end to what had started as the Great American Dream. Through brilliance and hard work a poor boy had risen almost to the presidency of General Motors. He had then left it for ethical reasons, only to fall victim to his own apparent lapse in ethics.

Duesenberg

Duesenberg! The name has a cadence all its own, almost a magical quality. And well it should be-cause the Duesenberg was arguably the mightiest motor car ever built in the United States.

But its fame was not confined to the new world. This automobile ranked among the very best anywhere and could stand with pride alongside the Hispano-Suiza and Bugatti of France, the Isotta-Fraschini of Italy, the Mercedes-Benz of Germany, and the Rolls-Royce of England. Although the car was invented in Europe, America had produced one that was equal to their very best.

And what about its American contemporaries, cars like Cadillacs, Lincolns, Packards, Chryslers,

1929 Duesenberg J LeBaron.

– RICHARD SPEIGELMAN

Duesenberg. When the advertisements said "He drives a Duesenberg," which they did, they said it all.

And just as the name Edsel would become synonymous with failure, Duesenberg would add its own term to our language, although at the other end of the scale. "It's a Duesie" became a metaphor to describe something superlative.

The Duesenberg story in the U.S. started when Fred and August Duesenberg's parents brought their young family to Iowa from Germany late in the 19th century. Being mechanically talented, Fred went into the bicycle building business.

Pierce-Arrows and Marmons? Fine autos to be sure, but not really in the same class as the J and SJ

When this failed the brothers joined the Mason Motor Car Co. of Des Moines, Iowa, as engineers.

By 1913 Fred and August were able to get into engine manufacturing, founding the Duesenberg Motor Co. in St. Paul, Minn., to build marine engines and racing cars. Their racers were so successful that by 1916 they had received the financial backing to set up the Duesenberg Motors Corp. with a plant in Elizabeth, New Jersey. With World War I raging, they built aero engines and other military equipment until peace came.

In returning to civilian production, the brothers wanted to switch from building four-cylinder engines to eights. Their backers disagreed, so the plant was sold to Willys-Overland and the pair soon found themselves back out west in Indianapolis in a new company called the Duesenberg Motor Co.

The first Duesenberg passenger car, the Model A, was introduced in 1920. It had a straight-eight engine and hydraulic brakes, both firsts in American production cars. A delay caused by a change from horizontal overhead valves operated by long, vertical "walking beam" rocker arms, to an overhead camshaft delayed the sale of the Model A until 1922.

The Model A was a good car and the Duesenbergs continued building a solid racing reputation, including winning the French Grand Prix in 1924, '25, and the Indy 500 in 1921, and '27. Despite this there were always financial difficulties. The company was reorganized in 1925, and the next year Errett Lobban Cord, president of the Auburn Automobile Co., gained control of Duesenberg.

Cord was a good businessman, a skill the Duesenbergs lacked; they had always been employees, not principles, in their various enterprises. Cord was also a man of vision, and the '20s were booming. He instructed the Duesenbergs to design a super car, one that could equal, yes even surpass, the world's finest. No better assignment could have been set before men of their talents.

By 1928 the design was completed, and in December the mighty Model J Duesenberg made its debut at the New York Auto Show. The automobile world would never be the same.

The J and the supercharged SJ, which came in 1932, were the cars that would establish Duesenberg as one of the world's great cars, and relegate the Model A Duesenberg, as good as it was, to the shadow of being a perpetual bridesmaid.

The normal J rode on a wheelbase of 142-1/2 inches (3619 mm). Its broad molybdenum frame rails were held together by six crossmembers. Some chassis were also built on a 153-1/2-inch wheelbase to accommodate larger bodies.

A couple of shorter, 125-inch (3175 mm) wheelbase, special-order cars were made for Hollywood actors Clark Gable and Gary Cooper.

These were called SSJs (short, supercharged J), although this was not an official factory designation.

As sturdy and refined as the chassis was, the *pièce de résistance* was under the hood. The engine was of almost racing specifications - a straight eight with four valves per cylinder operated by two chain-driven overhead camshafts. It displaced 420 cubic inches (6.9 litres) and measured some four feet (1.2 metres) from fan to flywheel. The apple green cylinder head was topped by polished aluminum cam covers.

As well as being an object of beauty, this powerplant was also a paragon of performance. Peak horsepower was 265 for the regular engine and 320 when the supercharger was fitted, a figure said to have been increased to nearly 400 under August Duesenberg's skilled hands. (Fred died in a car crash in 1932 after designing the SJ).

Top speed was claimed to be 116 mph (187 km/h), with 90 (145) available in second gear of the three-speed transmission. The supercharger upped these figures to 129 mph (208 km/h) top and 104 (167) in second. Acceleration was quoted as zero to 100 mph (161 km/h) in 17 seconds, this for a car that weighed close to three tons!

Duesenberg buyers usually contracted with one of the great coachbuilders such as Locke, LeBaron or Murphy to fit it with a body; the chassis were also favourites of European coach-builders.

Duesenbergs, therefore, came with a wide variety of styles and features. The J was built until 1937, right through the depths of the Depression, with a total of 470 produced.

The Duesenberg stands as a grand example of man's ingenuity, a mechanical artifact the likes of which will never be built again. It was the greatest American automobile of its era, and remains an almost priceless collectible today.

EDSEL

No word in the recent automotive world exemplifies failure quite as powerfully as does Edsel, the medium-priced car built by the Ford Motor Co. from 1957 to '59. The Chrysler/DeSoto Airflow models perhaps come closest, but having been built in the mid-30s, memories of them are fading.

The genesis for the Edsel could, if one were prepared to take a little poetic licence, be traced back to before World War II, to the evolution of the power of General Motors. GM president, Alfred P. Sloan, Jr., had cleverly crafted a hierarchy of cars designed to lure buyers up the success ladder from Chevrolet through Pontiac, Oldsmobile, Buick and ultimately - if they achieved real success - to the status of a Cadillac.

1959 Edsel.

dent in 1919, observed the wisdom of the GM strategy. As early as 1922 he convinced his father that they should expand their line from their single model, the venerable Model T.

Thus, Ford added a luxury car by buying the ailing Lincoln Motor Co. that year, and introduced a more affordable version called the Lincoln Zephyr for 1936. In 1939, the corporation added the Mercury, really a deluxe Ford, to further fill out its offerings.

Following the war (Edsel died in 1943), the Ford Motor Co., which was in a shambles because of old Henry's autocratic management, came

Edsel Ford, the original Henry's only child who became the Ford Motor Co.'s titular presi-

82

under the stewardship of Edsel's son, Henry Ford II. HFII engaged an ex-military brain trust known as the "Whiz Kids" and was able to nurse the company back to health. Its all-new 1949 model was a sensation and is credited as "the car that saved the company." Ford now seemed to be on a roll, and it brought out the sporty and successful two-passenger Thunderbird in 1955.

At about the same time, Ford management - still aspiring to go model for model with GM - decided that it needed more strength in the middle of the market to compete with the Pontiac, Oldsmobile and Buick from GM. There were also Dodges and DeSotos from Chrysler vying for the same customers.

This was the genesis of the "E-car," as it was coded, and it was decided that the project should go ahead. All the signs for such an entry looked good, although some within the company questioned the need for another medium-priced car; Ford already had the Mercury, and also its corporate clone the Monarch in Canada.

But the naysayers were overcome. Optimism was strong, memories of World War II and Korea were fading, and in 1955 Detroit enjoyed its best year in history to date.

To demonstrate its seriousness about the E-car, Ford established a separate division for it. First year production was confidently projected as 200,000, and five plants were to be established to build them. Although the new car

wouldn't appear until the fall of 1957 as a '58 model, public announcements began as early as August 1956.

A new car needed a new name, of course, so Ford launched an extensive name-the-car program. The creative juices began to flow, and among some 8000 possibilities came such gems as these from a New York poetess named Marianne Moore: Resilient Bullet, Mongoose Civique, Varsity Stroke, and even the Utopian Turtletop.

Also among the finalists were Ranger, Pacer, Corsair and Citation. Although these names would later be used as series designations, they were not considered expansive enough for the car itself. Finally, after deciding that the dignity of the company could not quite stand the Mongoose or the Turtletop, the name Edsel, suggested very early but vetoed by the Ford family, was raised again. After much persuasion, family objections were overcome and the car became the Edsel.

Meanwhile, an important change was taking place in the automobile market. Fords, Chevs and Plymouths were getting larger and creeping into the medium-priced market where they were eating into sales in that segment. In 1957, the sales of Chrysler's DeSoto, which was only four years away from extinction, were off more than 50 percent, followed by Mercury and Dodge which were just about as bad. Buick and Oldsmobile were down significantly, too.

To complicate the situation, by the time the

1958 Edsel was introduced in September, 1957, a short but sharp economic recession was getting under way, which further eroded demand for medium-priced cars. It was a far cry from optimistic 1954 when the project had been conceived.

Then there was the matter of styling. Although in retrospect the Edsel's general styling, compared with the chrome-laden GM cars, was tasteful enough, most people didn't get past the front end. This was, unfortunately, dominated by a three-piece grille, the most prominent feature of which was an oblong, vertical opening with a smaller egg-shaped insert.

The grille was quickly dubbed a "horse collar" or - even worse - "an Oldsmobile sucking a lemon."

Other factors were against the Edsel, too. Buyers weren't thrilled with the transmission selector buttons in the steering wheel hub. And the Edsel suffered some quality problems because it did not yet have its own production facilities; it had to be built on established Ford and Mercury assembly lines, inserted in among the regular models. Line workers didn't welcome having to assemble this misfit which not only uses different parts, but added an extra car per hour to their work load.

The result of all this was that instead of the hoped-for minimum 100,000 sales of the '58 Edsel, only 63,110 '58s were built. The car was already on its way to becoming a failure.

In an attempt to perk up sales for 1959, the line was simplified by dropping the Pacer and Citation, leaving only the Ranger and Corsair. The horse collar grille was softened, and a six-cylinder engine was available rather than just V-8s. There was no turning it around, however; model-year sales declined to 44,891.

Although a restyling was done for 1960, which replaced the ill-fated grille with a split type resembling the Pontiac's, the Edsel was really finished. Production ended on Nov. 19, 1959, after only 2846 of the '60 models had been built.

Ford had been caught in the crossfire of several factors: a declining medium-car market; a recession; some quality problems; and generally unacceptable styling.

The Edsel was not significantly worse than its competitors; it just couldn't overcome these forces. Its name is now inextricably linked with failure.

FORD MODEL T

The Model T Ford was more than just the steel, rubber, wood and glass that went into it; it was a legend, a social phenomenon that, more than any other single development, liberated North America, and other parts of the world too. It was a true "people's car" long before the term had been applied to the German Volkswagen.

It brought personal transportation into a price range that most people could afford and by so doing, reduced isolation and turned us into a mobile society. It expanded the average person's private travel horizon from animal scale, how far a horse could travel in a day, to machine scale, which was magnitudes greater.

In addition to being a social phenomenon,

1909 Ford Model T.

– FORD MOTOR CO.

Model T era Ford defeated the monopolistic Selden patent that had been hobbling the industry (1911), introduced the assembly line to the building of cars in (1913), and instituted the $5 day (1914).

Henry Ford had always been interested in light, uncomplicated cars. The first vehicle he built in 1896, his Quadricycle, was small and simple, and ran on little more than bicycle wheels. When he was finally able to get his successful Ford Motor Co. going in 1903, (the third automobile enterprise he was involved in) with the financial assistance of Detroit coal

the T and Henry Ford also contributed significantly to industrial development. During the magnate Alexander Malcomson, that was the type of car he favored.

The first car offered by the new company, the Model A, followed this pattern. It was a light, two-passenger runabout of which, according to Ford's official figures, 670 were sold.

But Malcomson preferred heavier vehicles, and he was putting up a good part of the money, so that's the direction the company started to go. As the models marched through the alphabet, many of the cars got bigger engines and longer wheelbases; by 1906 the Model K was a rather expensive ($2500) six-cylinder automobile.

Henry's heart wasn't in it however, and when he was finally able to shake free of Malcomson's grip (the coal king sold his Ford Motor Co. shares in 1906), Ford turned back to the simple sturdy design he loved.

Models N, R, and S of 1906-07 were much closer to Henry's philosophy. Drawing on the pattern making genius of Charles "Cast Iron Charlie" Sorensen, the Danish-born craftsman who was devoted to cast iron, and could carve wooden casting patterns from simple descriptions (Henry wasn't much for blueprints), Ford was able to move ahead quickly with his dream. Sorensen had joined Ford in 1905 and was to become, over a 39-year period, not only a tower of strength for the company, but Henry's staunchest aide.

Henry had recently discovered something that he wanted to incorporate into his cars too: heat treated vanadium alloy steel. This product was being used in European cars, and when Henry found a small steel company in Canton, Ohio, that could manufacture it, vanadium steel was gradually worked into the Model N Ford. It would be a key ingredient in the Model T.

The stage was set to pursue Henry's vision. In the winter of 1906-07, Henry asked Sorensen to partition off a room on the top floor of the Piquette Ave. plant and put a good lock on the door. There, Henry, Sorensen and a few trusted associates designed the Model T.

Henry was not a trained professional engineer but he had an uncanny instinct for knowing what would work. The Model N engine had its four cylinders cast separately. For the Model T, however, Henry wanted them incorporated into a single cylinder block.

Sorensen struggled with the design without much success, working with the then conventional closed-top cylinders. Henry cleverly suggested that they slice off the top of the block, and transformed the way engines were built. The detachable cylinder head that resulted had alleviated Sorensen's task. And because the block was open at both ends, machining and servicing were greatly eased.

Fuel ignition was another challenge that was met ingeniously by fitting horseshoe-shaped magnets to the flywheel to create a powerful magneto. Once started - by a small battery for ignition (by cranking, of course - there was no electric starter yet) - the Model T engine magneto generated its own ignition spark.

Henry didn't trust the sliding gear transmissions and vicious clutches of the day. He specified a planetary gear transmission - the same principle employed in today's automatics - which used bands and clutches operated by two foot pedals. That made the task of learning to drive simpler because the driver didn't have to shift gears with a conventional gear lever and clutch.

To move off, the driver pushed the left (high-low; it was only a two-speed transmission) pedal halfway down to get neutral, moved the handbrake, which operated the rear wheel brakes, all the way forward, and then pushed the left pedal right down to engage low gear. When sufficient speed - say 10 mph - had been reached, the driver simply allowed the left pedal to move all the way up through its mid-point neutral position into high gear. For reverse the middle pedal was depressed. The brake pedal, which operated on a transmission band, was on the right. Neutral could also be obtained by moving the hand brake lever to its mid-point.

While this may sound a bit complicated in the telling, the operation really wasn't, and new drivers were soon able to make gentle starts and smooth shifts. The pedal-operated transmission also enabled the driver to easily rock the car back and forth if it got stuck in the terrible, muddy roads of the day.

Steering was another novel idea on the Model T. Instead of mounting a steering gearbox at the bottom of the steering column as others did, Henry had a small planetary gearset fitted right under the steering wheel. The steering was very heavy, but it also meant that the steering wheel could be easily removed, allowing some of the most hilarious Laurel and Hardy movies scenes ever filmed ("If you don't like the way I drive, you drive..." and the wheel was handed over).

The Model T debuted late in 1908 as a 1909 model. It was all that Henry had hoped it would be, and it was a fantastic success. With a top speed in the order of 45 mph (72 km/h), fuel economy of 20 to 25 mpg, and a simple but sturdy design with plenty of road clearance, it was exactly what was needed. The more Model Ts he sold, the lower Henry dropped the price, until it reached $295.

When Model T production ceased in 1927 more than 15 million had been produced, a mark that wasn't exceeded by a single design until the Volkswagen Beetle did it in 1972.

Henry's beloved Model T Ford had, more than any other car, put North America on wheels, and irreversibly changed its whole way of life.

FORD MODEL A
1928-1931

1930 Model A Ford Roadster.

– BILL VANCE

Henry Ford I was a stubborn man. Once he got his beloved Model T into production in late 1908, an invention he considered to be the perfect car for the masses, he wasn't about to stop making it. Thus, even though sales were flagging in the 1920s, and others offered more in luxury and style, autocratic old Henry hung on to the Model T.

Finally, however, an end had to come for the ubiquitous Ford. Even with the introduction of changes like balloon tires, and optional wire wheels in the mid-20s, unsold stocks began building up on dealer lots.

In 1926, when sales fell by more than a quarter-million units, it finally became apparent to Henry that foot-shifted transmissions, questionable brakes and his spartan approach to motoring could no longer meet the competition.

In May of 1927, following 19-years and more than 15 million Model Ts, it was announced that they would no longer be built. The car that had pioneered the use of the moving automotive assembly line and the unprecedented Ford $5-a-day wage rate, was finally going out of production.

What could possibly replace it?

Henry had been so dedicated to the Model T that he had allowed only minimal preparation for its replacement. It seemed as though he really didn't want to face the reality of giving up

88

the famous Tin Lizzie. Thus, when Highland Park and the giant River Rouge plants stopped churning out Ts, some 60,000 workers were thrown out of jobs, and Ford dealers had no new cars to sell. They had to survive for almost nine months on providing parts and service for Model Ts.

But if there was trouble in dealerland, there was also strife in the Ford family that would slow the new car's introduction more than necessary. Charles Sorensen, production chief and a close ally of Henry Ford's, said in his book *My Forty Years With Ford* that development of the new car was delayed by differences between Edsel Ford, Henry's son and titular president of the company, and Henry, who actually controlled the company.

Edsel was an imaginative, forward-thinking man who wanted a well-appointed car with modern features, one that could go head-to-head with GM's Chevrolet. Henry, on the other hand, wanted to stay with, for example, the planetary transmission; he didn't believe the sliding gear ("crunch gear," he called it) transmission would stand up.

Finally a compromise was reached, and work on the new model proceeded at Ford's Dearborn, Mich., headquarters. Events then took place with startling speed. In *Forty Years*, Sorensen said: "Actually, when Mr. Ford decided to replace Model T, clearing the design and getting Model A (as the new car would eventually be called,

named after the first Ford) into production took only 90 days. But it was six months before Henry Ford would go to work."

With the almost-fabled reputation that Ford and his car had built up at home and abroad, it is probably safe to say that no new car in history has been so eagerly awaited. Rumors abounded. It was said that the new car would be a combination of a Lincoln, which Ford produced, and a Ford, and be called a Linford. It would be named after Henry Ford's close friend, Thomas Edison. It would look like style leader LaSalle or like a small version of the luxury Marmon.

Henry Ford revelled in the publicity and ordered a tight cloak of secrecy kept around the Model A's development. The anticipation mounted and, finally, in late November, 1927, Ford inserted a series of five daily advertisements in thousands of newspapers. On the fifth day of the series, the public was shown a picture of the Model A Ford.

When the car's first public showing took place in January, 1928, in Madison Square Garden, police lines had to hold back the surging mob of people eager to see Henry's new baby. Fifty thousand New Yorkers placed orders and paid deposits on new Fords. The mob scenes were repeated in other major cities at home and overseas. Ford had another winner.

Many of Edsel's ideas had prevailed. Apart from transverse leaf springs, the A had little in common with the T. The new car was powered by a 200.5 cubic inch (3.3 litre) side-valve four that was not only larger than the T's 176.7 (2.9 litre) unit, but was also, at 40 horsepower, twice as powerful.

It had four-wheel mechanical brakes instead of the T's two-wheel; a three-speed sliding-gear transmission rather than the foot-operated two-speed planetary; a foot-operated accelerator pedal in place of the steering wheel lever; a proper steering gearset in the steering wheel hub; and battery and coil ignition in place of the flywheel-mounted magneto. It even had lighted instruments on the instrument panel.

The Model A was not only mechanically superior to the T, it was also much more stylish. It, indeed, did bear some resemblance to the Lincoln and came in a wide variety of models.

Performance was also significantly better. Whereas the Model T could barely achieve a top speed of 45 mph (72 km/h), the Model A could sail well past 60 mph (96 km/h). In a simulated road test conducted by *Road & Track* magazine in its February, 1957, issue, it estimated a top speed average of 62 mph (100 km/h). And this was for a 1930 model; 1928s and '29s were said to be even faster due to larger wheels and a higher rear axle gear ratio.

The Model A was also quite spirited in acceleration. *R & T* placed its zero to 60 mph (96 km/h) time at 29.0 seconds, and noted that it was as quick to 60 (96) as a contemporary (1957) Volkswagen. The A's ability to reach 45 mph (72 km/h) in second gear was also lauded, a feature that helped the Model A achieve, as *Automotive Industries* magazine commented back when the A was new, "stoplight getaway (that) would embarrass the owners (and manufacturers) of even our highest-priced vehicles."

Production figures for the Model A would come out as 633,594 in 1928, 1,507,132 in 1929, 1,155,162 in 1930 and 541,615 in 1931. The severe drop in production in 1931, the Model A's last year, was no doubt largely a result of the Great Depression.

But there was also the stiffening competition from Chrysler and General Motors. Chevrolet, for example, had introduced its six-cylinder engine in 1929. And Chrysler's Plymouth, which came on the scene in 1928, featured hydraulic brakes and in 1931 received advanced "Floating Power" rubber motor mounts. There was also the rumor of Ford's own fabulous V-8 engine, which the company would introduce in 1932 to bring the performance and smoothness of eight-cylinder power to the low-priced field.

Although it was built for only four years, the Model A Ford was a popular car, a transitional step between Ford's ancient Model T and its modern V-8.

First Ford V-8

Henry Ford has the distinction of being the man who put North America on wheels. His Model T, of which more than 15 million were built from 1908 to 1927, was just the kind of car that was needed: sturdy, simple and cheap.

But the Model T that brought motoring to the masses was not the only Henry Ford legacy. He pioneered the moving automobile assembly line in 1913 and ushered in real mass production. The $5 a day wage he started paying in 1914 made it possible for the workers who built his cars to also afford to buy them.

While he did allow his Model T design to stagnate before replacing it with the Model A in 1928, Henry would make one last great contri-

1932 Ford V-8.

– Ford of Canada

bution to automotive engineering: the low-cost V-8 engine in 1932.

Although it would be many years before it was widely adopted, the V-type engine went back a long way. Arranging the cylinders in a vee formation had been recognized as desirable by a few pioneering steam-engine designers as early as the mid-19th century.

Even then it was noted that placing the pistons in a vee rather than in a line offered such advantages as compactness and a shorter, sturdier crankshaft. The internal combustion engine and the motor car came along later, of course, and there were a few innovative thinkers who also tried V-type engines in some of the very earliest automobiles.

Panhard-Lavassor of France had a car powered by a Daimler V-2 in 1891. Mors, another French company, is credited with having a V-4 in 1897, while the Ader company, also French, sold cars with V-2, V-4 and V-8 engines in the 1900 to 1904 era.

The French de Dion-Bouton was the first car to sell a series production V-8 engine in its 1910 model. This is said to have inspired Cadillac in America to move to V-8s for 1915, which it augmented with V-12s and V-16s in the 1930s.

When Henry Ford went from the Model T to the Model A in 1928, he had stayed with a four-cylinder engine. Arch-rival Chevrolet, however, stung Henry by coming out with a six in 1929, a powerplant that was smoother and more powerful than the Model A's.

Henry immediately made up his mind. "We're going from a four to an eight," he said, "because Chevrolet is going to a six." V-8s were not new to the Ford Motor Co. They had had one in its luxurious Lincoln car since it acquired the company in 1922.

Henry's approach was a novel one, however, in that he intended to make a low priced V-8 with a one-piece cylinder block. Up to that time V-8s had been made up of two or more pieces bolted together, which made them expensive and slow to produce.

In 1930, Henry selected three of his best and most trusted engineers, Emil Zoerlein, Carl Schultz and Ray Laird, to design his new V-8. For complete secrecy, he had them work in the replica of Thomas Edison's Fort Myers, Fla., laboratory located in the Ford Greenfield Village Museum in Dearborn, Mich.

Although Ford's fully equipped engine laboratory was just a stone's throw away, the engineers had to work in what were quite primitive conditions. When the design was completed, they struggled with the daunting task of keeping the 54 molding cores in place while they cast the intricate, one-piece cylinder block.

In desperation, they added pattern shop head Herman Reinhold to their team. With his assistance an engine was ready for testing by 1931, and they used Edison's overhead lineshaft as a kind of crude dynamometer, driving it with a long belt from a pulley on the end of the crankshaft.

With an engine that would run, the team set about learning how to mass produce it. Henry's closest aide, pattern making wizard, Charles "Cast Iron Charlie" Sorensen, was brought in. Overcoming his early prejudice toward the one-piece V-8 block, Sorensen threw all his efforts into the job. After much heartbreaking scrappage, around-the-clock toil, and many failures, the Ford V-8 gradually became a practical reality.

In early 1932, Ford announced publicly that he would produce a low-cost V-8 engine. As a little insurance against possible failure of the eight, and to satisfy loyal four-cylinder fans, an improved version of the Model A four, known as the Model B, would also be offered.

Ford needn't have worried. His name was still magic in the land, and when the new V-8 Model 18 (one-eight, for the first Ford V-8) was unveiled in April, 1932, it was a sensation. In spite of the dire economic conditions more than six million eager people came out to see this new Ford.

Although there were elements of the Model A in the styling, Henry's son Edsel had worked with Ford stylists to produce a quite pleasing design. A vertical strip grille hid the radiator, the fenders were nicely crowned, and horizontal accent striping gave the Ford a distinctly Lincoln-like appearance.

But the real story was under the hood. Here was a Ford with twice the cylinders of the famous Models A and T. It was a 221 cubic inch (3.6 litre) side-valve V-8 that delivered its 65 horsepower (Chevrolet's six had only 60) with nearly the smoothness of a turbine.

While the new V-8 delivered vibrationless, powerful driving, early ones were also plagued with problems. There was the usual scepticism of anything new, and the rumor soon started that "pistons lying on their sides will wear egg shaped." This was totally false, of course, but early oil consumption problems seemed to verify the belief. There were also some bearing failures and cracked heads. With these teething troubles, only 212,000 of the '32 V-8s were produced.

Gradually the Ford V-8's problems would be solved, however, and refinements and improvements came with each new model.

Ford V-8s dominated auto racing for many years, and the 1932 Ford V-8 became the quintessential hot rod. The V-8 engine would become the standard of the American industry for almost three decades, until dethroned by fuel economy concerns.

The Ford flat-head V-8 served millions of drivers until it was replaced with an overhead valve V-8 in the U.S. in 1954, and in Canada in 1955. It had brought the smoothness of V-8 power to the low-price field, and pointed the way to the future. For that accomplishment Henry Ford's last great engineering contribution has earned its own special place in automotive history.

FORD 1949

1949 Ford Tudor.

– RICHARD SPIEGELMAN

In the years immediately following World War II, the Ford Motor Co., like every other major domestic auto manufacturer, offered only thinly disguised versions of their pre-war designs. But we were a car-starved society and buyers were eager to have anything that was new, pre-war technology or not. You put your name on the waiting list and waited, and perhaps quietly slipped the dealer a little something to move you up in the queue.

But while the automakers all offered warmed-over designs, there were a couple of important differences that set Ford apart from Chrysler and General Motors in the post-war automotive era: weak management, and products that were more obsolete than those of the competition.

Henry Ford had appointed his only son Edsel as company president in 1918 at the age of 25. But while Edsel was the titular head, he was emasculated by Henry, who continued to make the major decisions and seemed to be doing everything possible to undermine Edsel.

Unfortunately, time had passed Henry by. He was locked into an austere Model-T mentality while Alfred P. Sloan, Jr., the brilliant engineer/manager at General Motors, was forging ahead with the annual model change and more comfortable vehicles. He was deftly slicing up the automotive market from the entry level

Chevrolet at the bottom, all the way up to the luxury Cadillac at the top.

Edsel was officially the president of Ford until his death in 1943, which was probably contributed to by the treatment he received from his father. On Edsel's death, old Henry assumed official power for a short while, but it was apparent that at the age of 80 he was not up to the job.

Something drastic had to be done if a Ford was to remain at the helm of the Ford Motor Co., so Henry Ford II, Edsel's eldest son, was pulled out of his navy training and made president. The mighty company was now in the hands of a young, inexperienced man, with Henry the First in his dotage and unable to provide much assistance.

Young Henry inherited his grandfather's closest aide, Harry Bennett, who had an unsavory reputation from his days as head of the Ford "Service Department" (company police), and had held undue influence over the elder Ford. Bennett had even expected to become president. One of Henry II's first significant administrative acts was to fire Bennett.

The other problem Ford had was its obsolete cars. Due to old Henry's stubbornness, Fords still had such features as a solid front axle and transverse-leaf "buggy springs" long after GM and Chrysler had switched to independent front suspension with coil springs. Another example of Ford's backwardness was that their cars hadn't been fitted with hydraulic brakes until 1939, while Chevies had had them since 1936, and Chrysler products had always been equipped with them.

The result of the engineering lag was that, after the war, the Ford Motor Co. was in dire need of a modern new design. The public would buy almost anything that was offered until the post-war shortage of new cars was satisfied, but by 1949 the bloom would be off. That's why a new Ford was critical.

Henry Ford II quickly recognized that he needed some new management talent in the company. Coincidentally, it was at about this time that a group of bright, young (26 to 34), well-educated officers came out of the armed services and decided to pool their skills to provide management consulting services.

When they sent young Henry a telegram suggesting that Ford might be able to benefit from their expertise, he invited them to Dearborn for a chat. A deal was consummated and that's how the "Whiz Kids" became part of the Ford Motor Company in 1946.

They were indeed a very capable group who would eventually all do well; six of the 10 ultimately became vice-presidents of Ford, two became president, and one of these, Robert McNamara, later became U.S. secretary of defence in the Kennedy administration.

With a strong management team in place,

the next requirement was a state-of-the-art product. In mid-1947 Ernest Breech, Henry Ford II's assistant whom he had hired away from General Motors in 1945, announced that Ford would have a new car for model year 1949. It was known that GM, Chrysler, Hudson and Nash were hard at work on new vehicles. And Studebaker had scooped them all with its new "coming-or-going" 1947 model. To meet the competition, the new Ford had to be ready by the summer of 1948, an extremely short development time.

In spite of the tight deadline the goal was accomplished. The solid V-8 engine was kept but everything else was new. A modern chassis was developed with independent coil-spring front suspension. At the rear, the single transverse leaf spring was replaced by two longitudinal "Para-Flex" leaf types.

The usual three-speed, column-shift transmission was used but, as was the custom at that time, the rear axle had a low "stump-puller" gear ratio. North American drivers were pretty lazy about shifting gears, automatic transmissions were not yet common, and the mark of a good car was its ability to "take the hills in high."

Manufacturers met this challenge by providing a combination that allowed motorists to do most of their driving in high gear. For those wishing more relaxed cruising, an overdrive unit was available. It was a popular option among commercial travellers who valued the extra fuel economy and quietness.

The job of styling the body of the new Ford went to an outside designer by the name of George Walker, formerly of Nash. This prompted Ford's own chief stylist, Eugene Gregorie, to resign from the company.

Walker came up with a truly trend-setting style. It was a complete envelope shape, symmetrical front and rear, with no hint of separate fender bulges; the fenders, hood and deck lid were all on one plane. The single horizontal bar grille was dominated by a large "spinner" in the middle.

The new style needed some getting used to, but it was a clean and attractive design and the public took to it quickly. They demonstrated their approval by buying over a million of them, more than double the sales of the 1948 Ford.

The 1949 Ford has been credited as the car that saved the company and, given the history, it's probably true. The Ford Motor Co. was now back on its feet and capable of going head-to-head with General Motors and Chrysler. It had thrown off the stigma of technical obsolescence and had an able management team in place.

The company was poised for the epic production battles that would occur among the Big Three in the 1950s.

FORD THUNDERBIRD

Two-Seaters 1955-1957

1957 Ford Thunderbird.

– BILL VANCE

North Americans fell in love with sports cars in the 1950s. The appearance of such sporty foreign machines as MGs, Triumphs, Jaguars and Austin-Healeys from Britain introduced an exciting new element to driving.

Here were vehicles that made little pretence at being utilitarian; their mission in life was to provide enjoyable driving, not just transportation.

True, luggage space was limited, weather protection was minimal and rides were often harsh, but sporting types were prepared to endure these for fold-down windshields, cutdown doors, four-speed transmissions and willing engines - features that really set them apart from the American appliances driven by

their neighbours.

There had been much earlier domestic sports cars like the Stutz Bearcat, Mercer Raceabout, and Auburn Boattail Speedster, but these had been beyond the affordability of most people, and thus had never really become very popular. It took the little English roadsters to light the sports car fire over here.

North American auto manufacturers quickly picked up this trend, and as usual, it was the smaller ones that were able to respond the quickest. Crosley Motors Inc., of Cincinnati, Ohio, brought out its Hotshot in 1949, a cute little bug of a sports car, but one too small to make much of an impact. Nash Motor Co. of Kenosha, Wis., was next with its lovely Anglo-

American hybrid, the 1951 Nash-Healey.

The first of the Big Three domestic manufacturers to produce a post-World War II sportster was General Motors with its 1953 Chevrolet Corvette. This was a somewhat tentative step, however; GM only made 300 of them in the first model year, and didn't commit to metal, choosing instead to use fibreglass for the bodies, a material that would eventually become a Corvette trademark.

With GM in the game, Ford wasn't about to be left behind. But its approach would be quite a departure from Chevrolet's. Whereas the Corvette was totally different from anything else in the model line, although it did borrow components from Chevrolet sedans, Ford chose to make the Thunderbird much more like a cut-down full-size Ford.

Chevrolet had been captivated by foreign sports cars to the extent that it emulated them by fitting the Corvette with drafty side-curtains and a flimsy fabric top. Ford, on the other hand, preferred to call its new 'Bird a "personal car" that gave up no creature comforts, and fitted it with wind-up windows and the amenities of its full-size siblings. It could be had with a hard or soft top. The seats also accentuated the difference; the Corvette had individual buckets while the Thunderbird was fitted with a bench seat.

Since Ford management insisted that the new model use as many existing parts as possible, it carried a strong family identity. The horizontal fender line was very characteristic of the full-size Fords, which had been totally redesigned for '55, and the headlamps and taillamps were drawn from Ford sedans. On the inside, the T-Bird instrument panel and hardware exhibited a strong resemblance to the big Fords.

Under the hood of the T-Bird was to be found Ford's corporate 292 cubic inch (4.8 litre) overhead valve Mercury V-8, which developed 193 horsepower when mated to the standard three-speed manual transmission (with over-drive available), or 198 when the optional three-speed "Ford-O-Matic" was ordered.

Ford's new two-seater was introduced late in 1954 as a '55 model and became an immediate hit. Whereas Chevrolet sold only 700 of its 1955 Corvettes, even though it now had the fabulous new Chevy overhead valve V-8, Ford sold 16,155 Thunderbirds.

In fact the dismal Corvette sales had General Motors on the verge of discontinuing it, but the introduction of the T-Bird convinced GM that it had to stay in the game.

A performance comparison with the '55 Corvette V-8 found the T-Bird wanting. In its July '55 road test, Road & Track magazine reported that the Corvette, in spite of being lumbered with GM's two-speed "Powerglide" automatic transmission, could sprint to 60 mph (96 km/h) in a quick 8.7 seconds, and reach a top speed of 116.9

mph (188 km/h). The Thunderbird, on the other hand, with its three-speed automatic, took 9.5 seconds to reach 60 (96), and could only manage 110.1 mph (177 km/h), according to *R & T* (March '55).

The Thunderbird was carried over into 1956 with the same body, although there were some changes. To provide more luggage space the spare tire was moved from the trunk to the rear bumper, "Continental" style.

A larger 312 cubic inch (5.1 litre) optional V-8 developed 215 hp with manual transmission, and 225 with automatic. Cowl vents were added for better cabin airflow.

For 1957 the basic theme remained the same, but again with some changes. A new attractive combination grille and bumper adorned the front end, and the trunk was stretched five inches, allowing the spare tire to migrate back inside, although the Continental style tire was still optional. By this time the fin craze had hit Detroit, and little canted blades sprouted from each rear fender of the '57 T-Bird.

The bigger news was under the hood, however, in the form of supercharging. The 312 cubic inch V-8 could now be had with an optional Paxton-McCulloch, belt-driven centrifugal supercharger that increased horsepower to 300.

Power for the base 292 engine was now also up to 212, and the normally aspirated 312 developed 245, although a few modified versions

put out more. The supercharged 'Bird would prove to be very rare, with only 208 being produced, and is now the most collectible of two-seater T-Birds.

Although it had a good year, selling 21,380 '57 Thunderbirds, this would prove to be the last of the two-seaters. Ford management, especially Ford Division's austere general manager, Robert McNamara, one of the "Whiz Kids" who had joined the company right after World War II, had decided that there was more money to be made in four-passenger Thunderbirds.

GM and Ford, therefore, took divergent paths with their sporty cars: the Corvette became a true sports car, and the Thunderbird evolved into a large "personal luxury" car.

McNamara would be proved correct. The larger Thunderbird would go on to earn far more money for Ford than the Corvette would for GM. But two-seater T-Bird aficionados never forgave him, and mourned the passing of the "real" Thunderbird.

FORD MUSTANG 1965

1965 Ford Mustang.

– FORD OF CANADA

It could be plausibly claimed that the inspiration for the Ford Mustang came from General Motors. When the Big Three automakers - GM, Ford and Chrysler - brought out their 1960 compacts to "drive the imports back to their shores," they turned out to be quite distinct cars.

Ford's Falcon was a starkly simple plain vanilla vehicle. Chrysler was a little more daring with its "European-styled" Valiant. General Motors was the most innovative; the Chevrolet Corvair had an air-cooled pancake engine, which was different enough, but to add to the novelty they mounted it in the rear of the vehicle, à la the Volkswagen Beetle.

Alas, there seemed to be little reward for engineering imagination, and initial Corvair sales were poor compared with those of the Falcon. In an attempt to salvage the situation, Chevrolet decided to switch the focus of the Corvair from "family practical" to "sporty fun."

Chevrolet therefore brought out a 1960-1/2 version dressed up with such items as bucket seats and fancy wheels, called it the Monza, and sales took off. GM had tapped into a market segment where the Corvair's mechanical innovation was accepted and appreciated. And in the process they had identified a whole new youth oriented marketing niche.

The folks over at Ford observed all of this,

marvelled at how GM had turned disaster into victory, and set about considering how they could produce a competitor for the Monza.

Unfortunately for Ford's product planners, the mood in the board room had gone considerably conservative. Senior company officials were still smarting over the Edsel debacle, which had not only been a colossal public embarrassment, but had also left a large splash of red ink on Ford's ledger. They were gun-shy to say the least, and Henry Ford II wasn't ready to authorize any big expenditures for product development.

In spite of the constraints, the planners and stylists worked away under the direction of newly appointed styling vice-president Gene Bordinat to try to find an economical way to counter the Monza. The idea they came up with was to use the Falcon platform as a base, make the corporate 289 cubic inch (4.7-litre) V-8 optional, and clothe the whole thing in a sporty new two-seater body shell. The design that resulted had a low roofline, a short flat deck lid, and most importantly, emphasized its long hood.

A bright red clay model, then named Allegro, was shown to Lee Iacocca, head of the Ford Division, in the fall of 1961. With the unerring judgment of the good car man that he is, Iacocca immediately recognized it as a winner. He insisted, however, that they add two small seats in the rear. It was cramped, but it expanded the

car's market appeal to include young families.

But while Iacocca felt the design would be a marketing miracle, he still had to get chairman Henry Ford II to agree. Iacocca didn't obtain Ford's approval easily. In fact he had to resort to a little creative subterfuge to achieve it. According to Robert Lacey's book, *Ford, The Men And The Machine*, Iacocca presented Ford with extensive market research data which purported to reveal that a whole new "baby boomer" youth market had been uncovered. These would be the new car's buyers, a ready made clientele for this lusty, sporty car.

By the spring of 1962 Henry Ford was finally convinced, but only after he had added an inch to the length to make the back seat more habitable.

Others who were involved in the development of the Mustang, as it came to be named, inspired by a World War II fighter plane, deny that there was any such extensive early market research conducted. Donald Frey, who was manager of product planning at the time, was quoted in *Mustang Monthly Magazine* in May, 1983, as saying that "Most of the market research was done after the fact. They made it all up afterwards - somebody did - in order to sanctify the whole thing...The market research that you read {of} is a bunch of bull." And the Mustang's chief designer Don DeLaRossa is adamant that the design came out of his shop, not from any market research.

The Mustang was introduced to the public in April, 1964, as an early 1965 model. It had both six-and eight-cylinder engines available, was small and light, and handled well by the standards of American cars of the day. Lots of available options meant that buyers could have it in everything from "Plain Jane" to "Fast and Fancy" versions.

To say that it was a success would be a considerable understatement; it was a sensation. It struck a chord in the hearts of the young and the young at heart, and sold so fast that the Dearborn plant couldn't produce enough of them.

Fortunately for Ford it had the flexibility to utilize other plants and the one in San Jose was quickly converted to Mustangs. Even this wasn't sufficient, so a Falcon factory in Metuchan, N.J., had Mustang production added to it.

Both 1965 and 1966 model years saw Mustang production exceed half a million, a fantastic success for a new vehicle. The Mustang was virtually without competition and it established a whole new class of vehicle called the "pony car."

The success of the new model, plus the rare publicity of getting his picture on the cover of both *Time* and *Newsweek* magazines at the same time, did Iacocca's career no harm. In January, 1965, he was made Ford's vice-president, cars and trucks, while still only 40 years of age.

There is one Mustang vignette that has an interesting Canadian involvement. Someone was

either asleep at Ford, or the company had a terrible cash flow problem, because the first production Mustang, a white convertible bearing serial number 5F08F100001, somehow got onto a transporter and was shipped to St. John's, Newfoundland. There it was placed in the local Ford dealership showroom where it was promptly bought by Eastern Provincial Airline captain Stanley Tucker. By the time Ford realized its mistake, Mr. Tucker was happily tooling around the streets of St. John's in his new car.

Ford wanted that car back, but pleas and entreaties fell on deaf ears. Tucker continued to drive his Mustang for two years, rolling up a modest 16,000 kilometres (10,000 miles). Finally he succumbed, and traded it back to Ford for a loaded 1966 Mustang, the 1,000,001st produced. That first Mustang can be seen in the Henry Ford Museum in Dearborn, Mich.

FIRST HONDA CIVIC

It has been said that the Volkswagen Beetle was a terrible design brilliantly executed, while the British Motor Corp.'s Austin/Morris Mini that debuted in 1959 was a brilliant design poorly executed.

There is no question that the Mini, which pioneered the modern cross-engine, front-drive configuration, was a breakthrough in automobile engineering. Its creator, Alec Issigonis, deserves a permanent place of honor in the automotive hall of fame. He was, thankfully, recognized with a knighthood, becoming Sir Alec.

I happen to believe that Dr. Ferdinand Porsche, designer of the Beetle, also deserves his place in that same hall of fame, but that is a story

Honda Civic (1st Generation).

— BILL VANCE

could say that the Honda Civic was a better Mini, what the Mini should have been.

The Honda Civic appeared on the automotive scene in 1973, only 11 years after the Honda Motor Co. Ltd. of Tokyo had built its first car. Honda was the world's leading motorcycle manufacturer when it decided, in the early '60s, to try its hand at cars. Its first efforts were pretty basic by North American standards, consisting of tiny vehicles powered by engines of 360 and 500 cc displacement. Nevertheless, they were well accepted in Japan and soon Honda was planning

for another time. If we are prepared to accept the brilliant design/poor execution theory, we

The Honda 600s that arrived in North America in the early '70s were tiny coupe and sedan models powered by twin-cylinder, air cooled engines driving through the front wheels. After their excellent fuel economy was acknowledged, there wasn't much more of a positive nature that one could say about their suitability for our driving conditions. Honda realized this and set to work on a model with greater international acceptability.

Honda had been lucky in 1960 when it convinced the powerful Japanese Ministry of International Trade and Industry to allow it to move into four-wheel vehicles. MITI had been attempting to strengthen Japan's auto industry by consolidating the existing car manufacturers into three strong and diversified companies. The Honda MITI proposal was defeated, much to Honda's relief, and the company was able to launch into the four-wheel business, after having been so successful with motorcycles.

Honda's good fortune didn't run out when it received MITI's approval to build cars. By a stroke of luck the arrival of the Civic in North America coincided with the first so-called oil crisis of the '70s.

In October, 1973, on the eve of Yom Kippur, the most holy of Jewish holy days, Egypt attacked Israel. Israel retaliated and was eventually victorious, thanks to U.S. support. This so humiliated the Arab world that it struck back with the only weapon it had: oil. It embargoed oil shipments to the West and before it was over, the price of oil had quadrupled from about $3 (U.S.) a barrel to $12.

North America, particularly the United States, panicked. There were long line-ups at the gasoline pumps, and even reports of violence in the queues. Motorists were more concerned about the supply of motor fuel than they were about price, although they certainly grumbled about how much it cost.

It was a very propitious time to come on the market with a small, fuel-efficient car, and that's exactly what Honda had. That first energy scare really shot Honda into the automotive limelight, and made tiny cars truly acceptable.

Although not as small as the Mini, the Honda Civic was still a very diminutive vehicle. But within its over-all length of 139.8 inches (3551 mm), and width of 59.1 inches (1501 mm), it could accommodate four passengers and a reasonable amount of luggage. The wheelbase of only 86.6 inches (2200 mm) meant that rear legroom was snug, and taller than normal passengers would find their heads brushing the roof. But there were compensations. The hatchback with its fold-down rear seat provided an enormous 20.7 cubic feet of cargo space when there were only two passengers, making the Civic a very utilitarian vehicle.

As in the Mini, the Civic's engine was posi-

104

tioned transversely between the front wheels, although its transmission was mounted on the end of the engine, not in the sump as in the Mini. The 1170 cc (71.3 cubic inch) overhead cam four drove the front wheels through a four-speed manual transmission. With its 50 horse-power the 1610-pound (732 kg) Civic could, according to *Road & Track* magazine's testers (5/73), accelerate from zero to 60 mph (96 km/h) in a respectable 14.1 seconds, and reach a top speed of 91 mph (145 km/h).

But motorists weren't buying Civics for performance, although they did delight in zipping through tiny holes in traffic, parking on the proverbial dime, and shifting the buttery-smooth transmission. What they were really buying was economy, and again according to *Road & Track*, they got it. *R & T* reported that fuel consumption averaged 30 mpg (36 Imperial) in normal driving.

The Honda Motor Co. was clearly on its way in the four-wheel world. And the Civic was to prove that the Japanese engineers were a force to be reckoned with, that they could do more than just design a good little economy car.

In the early '70s auto emission standards were being established in North America. American automakers were complaining bitterly that they were being forced into fitting expensive catalytic converters and other power-robbing devices to meet these standards.

Honda set to work on the problem and came up with a low-pollution engine with three valves per cylinder. They called their system, rather grandly, Compound Vortex - Controlled Combustion (CVCC), and when tested by the U.S. Environmental Protection Agency in 1973, it comfortably met all of the pollution standards without a converter or other add-on hardware.

When our domestic industry engineers countered that this was easy enough to do on a small four-cylinder engine, but that it wouldn't work on Detroit's large powerplants, Honda quietly took two 350 cubic inch (5.7 litre) Chevrolet V-8s, fitted them with the CVCC system, and proceeded to pass the EPA standards with those big American V-8s. There were some red faces in Detroit.

The Civic launched Honda into prominence in the automotive world, and the company has gone from strength to strength as a globally competitive automobile manufacturer. Dalton Ouderkirk of Toronto had a good eye for the future and began selling Hondas even before the Civic was introduced. A few years later, with a nice sense of history, he bought back the first Civic he had sold in June 1973. It's in excellent condition and can be seen at Dalt's Honda dealership in Toronto.

HUDSON HORNET

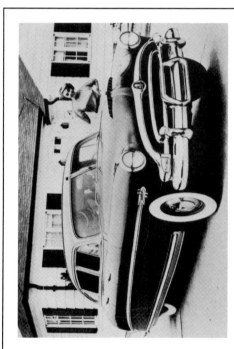

1951 Hudson Hornet.

– CHRYSLER CANADA

It is ironic that Hudson, one of the grand old names in North American automobiles, flashed with its greatest brilliance just before it died. Like a soaring meteorite that shines most brightly prior to crashing, it had saved the best for last.

The Hudson that performed this feat was the 1951-54 Hornet, the Hudson that most people remember above all others. With its big six engine and low centre of gravity it was the king of the racing circuits for four years, humbling such formidable competition as Oldsmobile 88s, Cadillacs, Chrysler Hemis and Lincolns.

But speed was not new to Hudson. Shortly after J.L.Hudson, Detroit's biggest department store owner, underwrote the formation of the Hudson Motor Car Co. by some ex-Olds Motor Works employees in 1909, the fledgling firm was making fast cars. Its 1912 "Mile-A-Minute" Roadster came along when a guaranteed 60 mph (96 km/h) was a very high speed for a production car.

Hudson switched over totally to six cylinder engines in 1914. In 1916 it brought out its "Super Six," and in April of that year famed racing driver Ralph Mulford piloted one to a one-mile stock car record of 102.5 mph (165 km/h) on the sands of Daytona Beach, Florida. This was followed up in May with a 24-hour stock record of 75.8 mph (122 km/h) at Sheepshead Bay, New York, and then in August Mulford set a new class record for the Pikes Peak climb.

Through the years Hudson prospered, developing a reputation for fast, sturdy cars. It added the low priced Essex in 1919 which led the way to popularizing closed cars. The Essex evolved into the good performing Terraplane in the thirties. Hudson reached the outstanding sales figure of almost 301,000 in 1929, which would turn out to be its all-time peak year. Although most of its cars were built in Detroit, it also had a Canadian operation in Tilbury, Ontario. Cars were built there from 1932 until World War II, and again after the war for a few years.

Hudson survived the Depression of the "Dirty Thirties," and in 1940 went on the hunt for speed records again, this time on the salt flats near Bonneville, Utah. In 1940 a stock Hudson driven by English record driver John Cobb (who would later become the first man to exceed 400 mph on land) captured just about every American Automobile Association (AAA) class record from one mile to 3000 kilometres, and from one to 12 hours. The 12-hour record was set at a blistering 91.29 mph (147 km/h) pace.

Following the 3-1/2-year industry shutdown during World War II, Hudson resumed production of slightly revised 1942 models. By 1948 it had its new offering ready, and it turned out to be a sensation. It was wide and low, thanks to what Hudson called "Step Down" design. This was achieved by dropping the floor pan

below the side members of the unitized body; traditional designs had the floor on top of the side rails. The result was a car that was only 60-3/8 inches (1534 mm) high, almost nine inches (229 mm) lower than the model it replaced. Tom McCahill, *Mechanix Illustrated* magazine's car tester, emphasized the Hudson's "worm scraper" profile by photographing its 64-inch (1626 mm) wide seat cushion standing on end beside the car.

Hudsons came in a variety of models with six and eight cylinder engines, and names like Commodore Six and (again) Super Six, and Commodore Eight and Super Eight. It was in 1951, however, that the bombshell Hudson would arrive in the form of the Hornet. Although really just a slightly revised Commodore on the outside, it was under the hood that the Hornet had its sting.

For the Hornet the Hudson engineers increased the bore and stroke of its already big six to 3.81 by 4.50 inches (97.8 by 114.3 mm), yielding a displacement of 308 cubic inches (5.0 litres), the largest six in the industry. It developed 145 horsepower at 3800 rpm in stock form, but the engineering department made available parts for "severe service," a coy way of saying racing, that could boost the six to close to 200 hp. Principal among these modifications was the "Twin-H-Power" dual carburetor set.

But even in stock trim the Hudson Hornet was pretty fast. *Road & Track* magazine tested one in 1951 and quoted a top speed of 93 mph (150 km/h), with a one-way run of 98 (158). McCahill and *Motor Trend* magazine both reported top speeds of 97 (156). Acceleration was also spirited, with *R & T* recording a zero to 60 (96) time of 14.5 seconds.

The combination of good handling brought by the low centre of gravity, and the hefty big six engine, made the Hornet a winner on the stock car tracks. In the hands of such aces as Marshall Teague and Tim Flock, Hornets were the undisputed champions of both AAA and the young National Association for Stock Car Auto Racing organizations. It would chalk up an astonishing 126 wins in four years.

But the old maxim "Win on Sunday, sell on Monday," didn't work for Hudson. In spite of the Hornet's prowess on the track, Hudson sales continued to fall, from 131,915 1951 models to 45,000 '53s. The introduction of the compact Jet in 1953, a belated restyling of its full size cars for 1954, and a lower priced Hornet Special weren't enough to stop the decline.

When it had become evident in 1953 that Hudson was on the ropes, negotiations began with Nash Motors of Kenosha, Wisconsin, a division of Nash-Kelvinator. This resulted in the amalgamation of Hudson and Nash, effective May 1, 1954, to form American Motors Corp.

The Nash products would prevail in AMC; Hudsons would continue only as re-badged Nashes until the name finally died in 1957. It was a sad end for an illustrious marque, but at least the Hornet had ensured that the last of the "real" Hudsons would go out in a burst of glory.

JAGUAR XK120

Two makes of cars can be credited with establishing the sports car market in North America following World War II: MG, and Jaguar. And while the first MG TCs were pretty basic pre-war designs with many limitations, the first post-war Jaguar roadster model to arrive here, the XK120, was both a styling and a mechanical tour de force.

Jaguar had been building sports roadsters before the war, the most famous of which was the SS100, but the company didn't carry the design over because it felt that an entirely new car was appropriate. Chief engineer William Heynes set about to design the mechanical components while the styling of the car fell to

1953 Jaguar XK120 Roadster.

– Bill Vance

trained auto stylist, Lyons had an uncanny ability to appreciate what made a car graceful and beautiful.

The engineering design parameters laid down for the new Jaguar were quite daring. Its engine was to develop peak power at a high 5000 rpm, which was surprising enough, but what was even more startling was that it was to be fitted with double overhead camshafts.

Twin overhead cams were not new, of course; Peugeot introduced them (and four valves per cylinder too!) in its Grand Prix racing car back in 1912. But their use had been confined almost

William Lyons (he became Sir William in 1956), co-founder of the company. While not a

109

exclusively to competition engines or expensive passenger cars such as Duesenbergs.

In addition to being sturdy and powerful, Lyons wanted the engine to be a thing of beauty, and few things are more beautiful to car buffs than the sight of two long polished cam covers held down by acorn nuts. And its power matched its aesthetic qualities.

Heynes came up with a 210 cubic inch (3.4 litre) inline six, which carried its massive crankshaft in seven large main bearings. It had a surprisingly long stroke for a post-war engine (bore and stroke were 3.27 by 4.17 inches, or 83 mm by 106 mm). Despite this it developed its 160 horsepower at a high 5200 rpm.

And if the engine was beautiful to behold, the car was even more so. Lyons outdid himself by creating a long sensuously flowing hood and fender line with the headlamps nestled in the valleys between the hood and fenders. He used a delicate vertical bar grille, and light bumpers that contributed more to style than they did to protection. The use of rear fender skirts provided a continuity of line that ran the length of the car.

The new XK120 Jaguar was introduced to the public at the Earls Court Motor Show in London in the fall of 1948. The model rotated on a large tilted platform and its impact on the crowd was electric. The motoring world was stunned; here was a car that was graceful and startlingly lithe of line, yet one that also promised outstanding performance from its 160-horsepower twin-cam engine. The 120 in its name had come from the top speed achieved by prototypes.

To add to the wonder of it all, the new Jaguar was priced at a modest 1275 pounds sterling, a figure so low that sceptics predicted it would never come to market for that, if it came at all.

Lyons and Heynes moved quickly to capitalize on the very favorable reception of the new Jaguar. In May, 1949, they took one to the famous Jabbeke highway in Belgium to demonstrate that the car had go as well as show. Fitted with an underpan and tonneau cover, and with the windshield removed, the XK120 more than lived up to its name by achieving a top speed of 132.6 mph (212 km/h), immediately becoming the world's fastest production car. Even in standard road trim it managed 126 (202).

That should have been enough to establish the new Jaguar's credentials, but Lyons wanted more. Under the influence of chief engineer Heynes who believed that the quickest way to prove a new model was in competition, a racing version of the XK120, the XK120C (for "competition"), was developed in just a few months.

A three-car team of Cs was entered in the 1951 Le Mans 24-hour endurance race in France. One of them beat the best the world had to offer by winning at an average speed of 93.49 mph. (150 km/h). It was a great day for Britain, and for Jaguar, which would go on to win five Le Mans races in seven years.

If more evidence of the Jaguar's durability was needed it came in 1952 when an XK120 coupe (a model introduced in 1951) was taken to a race track in Montlhéry, France. Here a team of crack racing drivers, including a young Stirling Moss, pounded the Jaguar around the Montlhéry circuit for seven solid days and nights. By the end of the week it had covered 16,862 miles (26,980 km), and averaged 100.31 mph (160 km/h), a truly remarkable demonstration of mechanical endurance.

When the XK120 arrived in North America, it established equally impressive performance figures. *Road & Track* magazine reported a top speed average of 121.6 mph (196 km/h), and zero to 60 mph (96 km/h) acceleration time of 10.1 seconds. Tom McCahill of *Mechanix Illustrated* recorded a zero-to-60 (96) time of nine seconds and a top speed of about 122 mph (195 km/h). He also reported that the Jag rode "like a bubble in a wash basin."

There were, however, some quality problems, a not unknown condition in earlier Jaguars, and the ever forthright Tom reported them too. It was, he said, "a rather crudely assembled job" that was "put together like a Chinese laundryman's version of a western sandwich."

The car he tested belonged to hop-up king, Andy Granatelli (later of STP fame), and in assessing its assembly quality, Tom concluded that "it would have been better if they had just shovelled the unassembled parts of the car I drove into an old bag and shipped them over parcel post."

But in spite of this, Tom was enthraled by the Jaguar and called it the finest high speed touring car in the world – high praise indeed.

And a touring car was what the XK120 was meant to be. Although it was raced, and even won occasionally, its real purpose was touring in the grand manner. Its greatest competition weakness was its brakes, which were prone to early fading under hard use. Its steering was also quite heavy, although it did handle reasonably well with its front torsion bar suspension.

In spite of some shortcomings, the XK120 Jaguar was, and still is, an extremely desirable car. It combined stupendous performance with stunning beauty at a reasonable price of under $5000. And its engine design, in various displacements, would last for almost 40 years.

During its six model-year run from 1949 to 1954, when it was replaced by the XK140, 7630 roadsters, 2678 coupes, and 1769 convertibles were produced. It is truly one of the benchmark cars in automotive history.

JAGUAR
Mark VII, VIII and IX

1953 Jaguar Mark VII.

– BILL VANCE

Most of our imported cars came from England in the late 1940s and early '50s. And the great majority of the sedans were small, resulting in names like "Baby Austin" and "Puddle Jumper." A few larger British cars like the Jaguar Mark V did come over, but they were fairly rare.

Then in 1951 we learned that English sedans (they call them saloons, but that has an entirely different meaning over here) need not be tiny and cramped. The arrival of the Jaguar Mark VII sedan (there was no Mark VI; Bentley had already used that designation) showed North Americans that a British car could be roomy, comfortable, elegant and fast, and still need not be in the Rolls-Royce price class.

The Mark VII had been unveiled at the Earls Court Motor Show in London late in 1950, and although it didn't create quite the sensation that the fabulous Jaguar XK120 had in 1948, it was warmly received.

Part of the Mark VII's excitement was that it was powered by the same awesome double-overhead cam in-line six-cylinder engine that propelled the XK120 roadster to its 120 mph (193 km/h) top speed. Although it displaced only 3.4 litres (210 cubic inches), a little less than a Chevrolet of the day, this six produced 160 horsepower, the same as the Cadillac V-8, and only 20 less than the sensational new Chrysler Hemi. And both of those engines displaced a

112

whopping 5.4 litres (331 cubic inches).

It's an interesting bit of Jaguar history that the double-overhead cam engine had really been intended to power a large sedan. The XK120 roadster had been developed only as a test bed for the engine, but it turned out so well that William Lyons, the guiding genius of Jaguar, produced the roadster first, a shrewd move as it turned out. Thus, the Mark VII represented the "real" home of this famous powerplant.

The Mark VII was nicely styled, a blending of traditional British lines into a spacious, modern envelope body. The front end, dominated by the beautiful vertical bar grille, was particularly appealing. It was a large car, riding on a 120-inch (3048 mm) wheelbase, and stretching 196 inches (4978 mm) in over-all length. It was no lightweight either, tipping the scales at 3960 pounds (1796 kg), almost exactly the same as the Chrysler Saratoga V-8 that *Road & Track* magazine tested in November, 1951.

In spite of its weight, and an engine that was considerably smaller than Chrysler's or Cadillac's, the Jaguar was no slouch in performance. *Road & Track* recorded a 0-to-60 mph (96 km/h) acceleration time of 12.6 seconds in its October, 1952, road test report, not as fast as the Chrysler Saratoga with the Hemi V-8, which took 10 seconds, but still very respectable.

The Jag was well ahead of the Lincoln Cosmopolitan (*R & T* March 1953), which did 0

to 60 in 14.4 seconds. And its luxury import competitors were no match for it either; the Mercedes-Benz 300 sedan took a leisurely 16.1 seconds to 60 (*R & T* April 1953), and the vaunted Rolls-Royce Silver Dawn took an even longer 17.0 seconds to 60 (*R & T* August 1953).

The Mark VII was pretty well the equal of the American cars in top speed too. *R & T* recorded a maximum of 104 mph (167 km/h), about the same as the Chrysler, although a little slower than the Lincoln's 108 (174). Again, its import competitor, the Mercedes 300, was slower, reaching only 98 mph (158). And in spite of being propelled by an engine whose horsepower Rolls-Royce loftily referred to as "adequate," the Rolls could achieve only a stately 88 (142).

In spite of its size the Mark VII proved surprisingly successful in racing and rallying. No less a personage than Stirling Moss won sedan races in one, and in rallying, Mark VIIs excelled in the daunting Monte Carlo Rally. Mark VIIs finished fourth and sixth in the 1952 Monte Carlo, second in 1953, and finally won the event in 1956.

In addition to having excellent performance, the Mark VII was very practical too. It could seat five or even six people, and had a large 17-cubic-foot trunk, obtained by fitting two fuel tanks and tucking them into the rear fenders. Two fuel fillers became a Jaguar trademark. And the traditional British wood trim and leather seats motto of "Grace, Space and Pace." While they didn't have the scorching performance, nor quite the panache of the glamorous XK series cars, they did establish the marque as a producer of high-performance luxury sedans, which are, of course, their bread and butter today.

could be found in the interior, along with such niceties as door-mounted tool trays.

North Americans welcomed Jaguars with open arms and at one point 96 per cent of Jaguar's output was slated for export. To cater to our generally lazier driving style, the Mark VII received an automatic transmission option in 1953 to supplement the four-speed manual. An electric overdrive was available with the manual gearbox from 1954.

The Mark VII was manufactured as 1951 to 1956 models, with the '54s to '56s designated as Mark VIIMs because of their more powerful 190 horsepower engine. For 1957 the Mark VIII appeared, the same basic car with minor changes which included a one-piece windshield and cutaway rear fender skirts, and now with 210 horsepower to propel it.

The last of the series, the Mark IX, came in 1959 with the engine enlarged to 3.8 litres, now producing 220 horsepower, and fitted with power steering and four-wheel disc brakes. By this time almost all of the big Marks came equipped with automatic transmissions. Production ceased in 1961 when the Mark IX was replaced by the more modern unit-construction Mark X. In 11 model years a total of more than 47,000 Mark VII, VIII and IXs had been produced.

The first big Marks were important cars for Jaguar, and they certainly epitomized Jaguar's

JEEP

1946 Jeep.

– CHRYSLER CANADA

There aren't many vehicle models that survived basically unchanged for over 40 years. In fact only two come to mind: the Volkswagen Beetle and the Jeep. The Beetle has, of course, been replaced by newer and better technology, but the Jeep soldiers on, with improvements admittedly, but still the same basic concept.

Even as it reached its 50th birthday in 1991, it was a tribute to the durability and soundness of the original design when Chrysler Corp. said that the Jeep, along with the new state-of-the-art Brampton car assembly plant, were the two jewels it obtained in its acquisition of American Motors in 1987.

The idea for the Jeep seems to have developed just before World War II, in 1937 or '38, when the U.S. military realized the need for a quick, versatile, go-anywhere vehicle - a kind of motorized cavalry horse. The ominous war clouds gathering over Europe added urgency to the matter.

The kind of all-terrain capability the Americans were seeking dictated four-wheel drive, a not unknown quantity because some heavy four-wheel drive trucks manufactured by the Four Wheel Drive Company of Clintonville, Wis., had been used in World War I.

The search for smallness in their new vehicle led the army to Butler, Pa., home of the American

115

Bantam Car Company, manufacturer of an American version of the English Austin.

Smallness they certainly found; the Bantam's wheelbase was a mere 75 inches (1905 mm), it weighed a feather light 1200 pounds (544 kg), and was powered by a 22-horsepower, 50 cubic inch (0.8 litre) four cylinder engine. After conducting some hill and dale testing, the army men concluded that, while the Bantam more than met the smallness criterion, it lacked enough performance and stoutness for their needs.

An ordnance technical committee in Washington finally agreed on the specifications for their new general purpose vehicle in June of 1940. A weight of 1300 pounds (591 kg) was specified, with a wheelbase of 80 inches (2032 mm).

It was to be capable of carrying a 600 pound (272 kg) payload, and most important of all, must have four-wheel drive. Four-wheel steering was even considered, and some prototypes were built with it, but the requirement was later abandoned.

Tenders were sent out to 135 American manufacturers, including all of the carmakers, inviting them to have a prototype developed in the almost impossibly short time of 49 days. A further 69 vehicles were to be ready 26 days later, a total of just 75 days.

Most companies looked at the tight deadline and dismissed the whole idea. Some, such as Ford, Chevrolet and taxicab maker Checker Motors, didn't formally bid, but did start experi-menting with such a vehicle. Only two companies, American Bantam, on the verge of bankruptcy and with nothing to lose, and Willys-Overland, submitted entries.

But Willys stated it could not abide by the time limits laid down. So it was almost by default that American Bantam got the contract. Willys went ahead anyway and developed its own version, which it called the "Quad."

American Bantam quickly realized its own baby car was too small to provide any of the components. It also knew that it needed help fast. By engaging the services of Detroit consulting engineer Karl Probst (the company didn't have a design engineer on staff!), and using a Continental engine, Studebaker axles, and a four-wheel drive design wheedled out of universal joint maker Spicer Manufacturing Co., the firm was able to meet the deadline.

American Bantam president Harold Crist and engineer Probst delivered the first "Bantam Recon Car" to the army at Camp Holabird, Md. at 4:30 p.m. on Sept. 23, 1940, a half hour within deadline.

The army immediately began a 30-day, 3699-mile (5800 km) shakedown test. There were problems, of course, but by the end of testing they were satisfied enough to give Bantam an order for 1500 of the versatile machines.

While all of this was happening the war in Europe was heating up. Hitler's Blitzkrieg was terrorizing the Continent, and U.S. military officials realized they would probably soon become involved.

If that happened they would need thousands of the little vehicles, not hundreds. They surveyed Bantam's production facilities and found them woefully inadequate. Despite all of the hard development work that Bantam had done, and to their bitter disappointment, the army had no choice but to find a manufacturer with larger capacity. Bantam did get to build the 1500, however.

That's how Willys entered the picture. In spite of not receiving the contract, they had, as noted, gone ahead and developed their own design, as had Ford.

Willys and Ford both offered the army their prototypes to test and the military had little choice but to take them up on it. The Willys model proved to be faster, thanks to its 61 horsepower car engine compared to the 46 that Ford got out of its tractor engine. The Willys was chosen as the official light military vehicle.

Willys-Overland got the big order for its design. But the army also had Ford build the vehicles under licence to Willys-Overland, and to Willys specifications. By the time World War II was over, close to 600,000 military Jeeps had been built; Willys-Overland had made about 360,000 and Ford the remainder.

How the Jeep got its name is always the subject of some specula-

tion seems to be that is was a simple contraction of GP, for general purpose utility vehicle. However it came about, it has now become almost a generic designation for light four-wheel drive utility vehicles.

The Jeep's ability to get into battle quickly, strike, and get out was invaluable. It was present at the important battle of El Alamein when Erwin Rommel's Africa Corps was defeated by the British. It performed yeoman service in Asia, the Soviet Union, the Pacific, and even China. It hauled ammunition and food, filled in as ambulance and rocket launcher, and even chauffeured generals around.

It was a magnificent part of the war effort, the cavalry horse that could go 60 mph (96 km/h) and didn't have to stop for wind. It is fondly remembered by soldiers around the world.

Following the end of World War II the Willys Jeep made a successful transition to civilian life, first as the Universal Jeep, then simply as the Jeep. Other models such as the sporty Jeepster, station wagons, and Jeep pickups in both regular and cab-over designs were produced. The Jeep, although designed for war, really came into its own in peacetime as the father of the modern 4X4 sport utility vehicle which is so popular today.

KAISER-FRAZER

1954 Kaiser Manhattan.

– BILL VANCE

American automotive historian Richard Langworth entitled his 1975 book on the Kaiser-Frazer Corp, *The Last Onslaught On Detroit*. Today, he might have called it *The Last American Onslaught On Detroit*, given what the Japanese have accomplished since the book appeared.

But during the period he wrote about - 1945 to '55 - Langworth was indeed correct; Kaiser-Frazer's was the only serious, and for a period successful, attempt by a new company to break into the Detroit automotive establishment.

When Henry Kaiser and Joe Frazer came together after World War II to form a car-building enterprise called the Kaiser-Frazer Corp., both were already successful entrepre-

neurs. Kaiser's fame came from his accomplishments as a construction magnate. His company had participated in building the mighty Hoover Dam and, during the war, turned out Liberty Ships.

Frazer started as a Packard mechanic and worked his way up through the industry to reach the presidency of Willys-Overland and then Graham-Paige. When K-F was formed, he controlled Graham-Paige Motor Corp., which, although it hadn't built a car since 1940, had been actively involved in war work.

These two men of action formed the Kaiser-Frazer Corp. in July, 1945, to challenge those established auto manufacturers who had managed to survive the Great Depression. The survivors

118

were the Big Three (General Motors, Ford and Chrysler) and the Little Four (Nash, Hudson, Studebaker and Packard). Crosley was also present, but it was so tiny, both in its cars and its production, that it hardly counted.

With no pre-war models to lean on, K-F had to design its cars from the ground up. There would be two nameplates for virtually identical cars: Kaiser, a popularly priced model, and Frazer, a more up-scale offering.

After an unsuccessful attempt at such advanced features as front-wheel drive, torsion bar suspension and unit construction, K-F settled on conventional body-on-frame, front-engine, rear drive cars. Stylist Howard "Dutch" Darrin came up with a full envelope design that was slab-sided in appearance and integrated the fenders into the body with a line that ran straight and level from front to rear.

It would be three years before Ford would be able to match that with its 1949 models. With a long 123.5 inch (3137 mm) wheelbase, the K-F provided between the axles seating, which gave ample legroom and a good ride.

To speed development and save money, the firm used a modified Continental industrial six-cylinder engine with 226 inches (3.7 litres) of displacement. This side-valve design developed 100 horsepower, and when there were some initial quality problems, K-F began manufacturing them itself under licence in 1947.

The K-F crew was able to have its first two cars ready to show by January, 1946. They were well received, and K-F acquired the huge Willow Run bomber plant near Detroit, Mich., and turned it into an automaking facility. Production was under way by June of 1946, and the cars were introduced as '47 models.

It was a good time to be selling cars because almost anything with wheels and an engine was sought after. The war had shut down auto production from 1942 to '45, and there was a huge pent-up demand for new cars. Kaiser-Frazer couldn't have started selling their very similar Kaisers and Frazers - the grille was the main difference - at a better time.

Things got off to a good start with total sales of more than 139,000 of the 1947 Kaiser and Frazer models. The 1948 cars saw few changes, and sales held at about the same level.

Competition had been increasing with the appearance of the all-new Raymond Loewy-designed '47 Studebaker, followed by the '48 "Step Down" Hudson. Then in 1949, the transition to post-war designs was complete with the Big Three's all-new styling and Nash's redesigned "Airflyte" series.

The result of the change to a buyer's market was that the combined sales of the '49-50 Kaiser-Frazers, still little changed, fell to just over 120,000 cars. Something had to be done, and stylist Darrin, who had left the company and then returned, was able to accomplish it. With the assistance of stylist Duncan McRae, he created the 1951 K-F line, coming up with one of the most beautiful designs of the '50s. Gone were the former boxiness and straight fenders, replaced by a low beltline with a gentle dip at the rear door, which followed the motif of the "Darrin Dip" at the top of the windshield.

Large windows, a nicely integrated grille, and imaginative interior-exterior styling made the '51 Kaiser a winner. There was a '51 Frazer too, but few were sold. After a disagreement with Henry Kaiser, Joe Frazer had left the company and the Frazer nameplate would soon disappear. With its new styling and the addition of a compact called the Henry J, K-F sales jumped to 231,608 for 1951.

The Kaiser had one serious disadvantage, however: the lack of a V-8 engine. The old side-valve 226 cubic inch six just couldn't match the performance and smoothness of its eight-cylinder competition.

Nineteen fifty-two was the beginning of the end for K-F's car-building efforts in North America - the firm also made vehicles in Toronto in 1950-51 - when sales dropped to 57,265. The following year they would be down to 46,398. Despite the addition of supercharging to the six in 1954 to raise horsepower to 140 from 118, just 10,097 were sold. A stylish fiberglass-bodied, sliding-door sports car, the Kaiser Darrin, was also offered, although few found buyers.

Only a handful of '55 models were built before production ceased and Henry Kaiser shipped the dies to Argentina where they were used to build a car called the Kaiser Carabela. Kaiser-Frazer's demise as a North American car builder marked the end of the last and bravest attempt by a new, home-grown company to crack Fortress Detroit. Many mourned its loss.

LASALLE 1927-1940

Although the LaSalle was built for only 14 years, it had a significant impact on the history of General Motors in particular and the auto industry in general. GM's legendary president, Alfred P. Sloan, Jr., launched the LaSalle in 1927 as a Cadillac Silver Anniversary car to fill the gap between Buick and Cadillac on GM's carefully nurtured hierarchy of prestige. It did, however, achieve more than that; it was responsible for the establishment of automotive styling departments as we know them.

The man behind the LaSalle's appearance was auto stylist Harley J. Earl. Earl was working for Don Lee, a Cadillac distributor and custom auto shop operator in Los Angeles in the 1920s. Lee counted

1927 LaSalle.

– BILL VANCE

among his clients many Hollywood celebrities who wanted something a little different.

To satisfy this desire, Lee employed Earl as a stylist to give the cars of the stars an individual touch. Earl was very good at his job, and he came to the attention of General Motors when Lawrence Fisher, general manager of Cadillac, was visiting the Lee operation.

So impressed was Fisher with Lee's stylist - he was not happy with the dumpy appearance of the Cadillac cars being designed by the Fisher Body Division - that he mentioned Earl to Sloan, and suggested that they have him do some work for Cadillac.

Sloan agreed, and Earl was invited to come to

Detroit on a short-term contract early in 1926 to style a new car, the LaSalle, that Cadillac was developing as a lower-priced "companion" car for the Cadillac. Earl's new LaSalle made its debut in March, 1927, and with nicely rounded curves, a low silhouette and imaginative two-tone paint, it was a sensation. GM had a winner on its hands and knew that it was due to Earl. The fact that Earl had borrowed liberally from the styling of the Spanish Hispano-Suiza luxury car didn't bother anyone, least of all Earl, who loved the styling of European cars.

He was almost immediately invited to join General Motors, reporting directly to Sloan, to set up what was called the Art and Colour Section. It was the beginning of formalized modern automotive styling, and the section increased in prominence and influence, later becoming the GM Styling Department.

The LaSalle made all of the vaunted Cadillac quality available at a more affordable price. It was powered by its own 303 cubic (5.0 litre) side-valve V-8 that developed 75 horsepower. To prove that the new car was more than just a pretty body, Willard "Big Bill" Rader, chief of Cadillac's GM proving ground experimental staff, set out to demonstrate the new car's durability. He drove a stripped down LaSalle for 10 solid hours, covering 950 miles (1530 km), and averaging an amazing 95.3 mph (153 km/h) in the process.

The new LaSalle was accepted immediately by the public. Total sales for the first two model years were almost 27,000, proving that the new car was being well received in the marketplace.

The 1929 model had its engine displacement increased to 328 cubic inches (5.4 litres), raising horsepower to 86. And along with Cadillac, it received the new synchromesh transmission for clash-free shifting into second and third gears. By the end of 1929, almost 50,000 LaSalles had been sold.

The next year saw yet another engine size increase, this time to 340 cubic inches (5.6 litres). By 1931, LaSalle and Cadillac were separated mostly by trim and identification, but with a price advantage of some $500 for the LaSalle.

By this time, the Great Depression was really starting to bite, and sales of cars, particularly expensive ones, were suffering badly. As a result, only 3290 of the lovely restyled 1932 LaSalles were sold.

Earl dramatically restyled the LaSalle for 1934, giving it "pontoon" fenders, bullet-shaped headlamps and "portholes" mounted on the side of the hood, a feature that would later become a famous Buick trademark. The engineers added such significant mechanical advances as hydraulic brakes and independent front suspension. Under the hood, the familiar Cadillac V-8 was supplanted by an Oldsmobile straight-eight for cost reasons. The new model, plus the easing economic conditions, contributed to LaSalle's 1934 sales more than doubling to 7218.

Changes for 1935 and '36 were largely cosmetic, although the fabric insert top was replaced by GM's new "Turret-Top" all-steel roof in 1935.

Despite sales increases to 8653 in 1935 and 13,004 in '36, there were new challenges for LaSalle. These came from two fronts: its own division in the form of the new Cadillac Series 60, and from the Packard Motor Car Co.'s Packard One Twenty, which had been introduced in 1935. Both were priced very aggressively, and both carried the prestige of established luxury car nameplates.

For 1937, LaSalle, with a V-8 back under its hood, fought hard to recover market share, and sales jumped to 32,005, its best year ever. Alas, that feat probably sowed the seeds of the LaSalle's demise because it was suspected that many of those sales came at the expense of its senior corporate sister, the Cadillac 60.

The LaSalle received a new body shell for 1939, but the marque was discontinued in mid-1940, its place on the GM ladder gradually having been squeezed out by higher priced Buicks and lower priced Cadillacs.

Although the LaSalle lasted only 14 years, and could technically be called a Cadillac failure, it did leave a lasting legacy. It, more than any other car, demonstrated that automotive styling was a critically important element in stimulating car sales. It resulted in the establishment of auto styling departments and raised automotive styling to a high art.

LINCOLN CONTINENTAL

Mark I 1940-1948

1940 Lincoln Continental.

— FORD OF CANADA

The original Lincoln Continental, now referred to as the Mark I, is considered a classic automobile design - more art than machine. It has been recognized for its outstanding aesthetic qualities by the New York Museum of Modern Art and others. It is somewhat ironic that it came about almost by accident.

The Continental really had two roots: a sports car designed by Ford Motor Co. stylist Eugene Gregory in the early 1930s, and the Lincoln Zephyr introduced as a 1936 model. Gregory's sports car didn't go into production but he never lost his desire to produce something different.

The opportunity came in the late '30s when Henry Ford's only son, Edsel, titular president of

Ford while old Henry still called the shots, wanted something sportier than the company was producing to drive on his winter vacation to Florida. Edsel, in contrast to his austere, nuts-and-bolts father, was a sensitive man who enjoyed the arts and appreciated the finer things of life.

Gregory took the challenge and set about to modify the Lincoln Zephyr into a thing of beauty. The Zephyr had been introduced as a junior Lincoln in response to the Great Depression, which had severely reduced the number of people who could afford large, expensive cars like the regular Lincolns with their massive V-12 engines.

124

It had a futuristic teardrop design with the headlamps molded into the fenders. In addition to being stylishly streamlined, it had some technically interesting features. It was built with unit construction and was the first car from Ford to have an all-steel top. It also offered an optional Columbia two-speed rear axle for quieter, more economical cruising.

The Zephyr was powered by a smaller side-valve V-12 engine than that of its large siblings. Ford engineers developed it out of the Ford V-8 by adding four more cylinders, but the engine did suffer some reliability problems, apparently due to poor oil circulation.

This was the car that Gregory used as the basis for Edsel's custom-built holiday car. The design started in the most basic way. Gregory told a Society of Automotive Engineers gathering in the 1980s that he had simply laid his paper on top of the Zephyr design and traced it out. He then added some of the styling features he had used in his original sportster to give the car its distinctive appearance.

For that "Continental" look, Gregory bobbed off the Zephyr's teardrop rear end, added a trunk and mounted the spare vertically behind it. He allowed the rear fenders to sweep back past the trunk, giving the vehicle a longer silhouette. He also lowered the car three inches (76 mm) and stretched the hood seven inches (178 mm). Fortunately, he kept the sensuously shaped Zephyr grille with its delicately curved narrow vertical bars. They decided to call it the Lincoln Continental.

The car that resulted was a magnificent design, so successful in fact, that when Edsel took it to Florida it was a great hit on the country club circuit. He is said to have come home with 200 orders for Continentals. That pushed Ford into production of a car that had begun as nothing more than a styling exercise for Edsel's personal car.

Continentals were produced in both hardtop coupes and convertibles, "cabriolets" as they were called for the true Continental flavor. Production only reached 350 coupes and 54 cabriolets in the first model year, 1940. For 1941, 850 coupes and 400 cabriolets were built.

The Continental was restyled for 1942, and in the opinion of many, lost much of the charm of the original. The vertical bar grille was replaced by a heavier appearing design with horizontal bars, the rear fender line was raised, and more chrome was added.

A larger 305 cubic inch (5.0 litre) 130-horsepower V-12 replaced the original 292 cubic inch (4.8 litre) 120-horsepower V-12, and was said to be more reliable. Only 200 coupes and 136 cabriolets were produced before domestic car production was shut down for World War II in February 1942.

After the war, production of the Continental

resumed. Like every other early post-war car, it was a slightly reworked version of the pre-war model. Unfortunately, the grille got even heavier and more baroque, and chrome trim was laid on with a more generous hand. Interestingly, they went back to the original 292 cubic inch (4.8 litre) V-12, but had managed to find five more horsepower to achieve a rating of 125.

In the 1946-48 era, 1943 coupes and 1391 cabriolets were produced before production of the Continental Mark I ceased. Despite calls for a new Continental, the Ford Motor Co. had more immediate and pressing matters on its hands, projects like bringing its new post-war Ford to market to save the company from the ruinous condition old Henry had left it in (he died in 1947).

It would not be until into the '50s that Ford would be able to afford the cost or talent to produce an all-new Continental (not a Lincoln Continental; the name stood alone). The new Continental Mark II appeared in 1956 and Ford created a separate division to produce it. Aimed squarely at the Cadillac, it was a beautiful car but it didn't sell well. Ford is reputed to have lost $1000 on each one, and for 1958 the Continental was shifted back to essentially a Lincoln body.

The Mark I Continental, particularly the 1940 and '41 model, is an almost legendary car because of its outstanding styling. Its mechanical components could only be described as mediocre, although its first and second gear ratios were quite high, and a favorite hot rodders' trick was to fit a Ford transmission with "Zephyr gears" to obtain higher speeds in the intermediate ratios.

In spite of the original Continental's classic status and low production, it has not, according to Dean Renwick, president of Antique and Classic Auto Appraisal Service in Mississauga, been as hot on the market as one would have expected. It may, therefore, be somewhat of a sleeper as a collectible. Its ageless beauty will, however, assure it of a permanent place in automotive history's hall of fame.

MERCEDES-BENZ 300SL

Imported car mega-dealer Max Hoffman of New York City sold everything from Volkswagens to Rolls-Royces in the years after World War II. He had a sense of what would sell and what wouldn't.

Hoffman became a Mercedes distributor in 1952, and when he saw the Mercedes-Benz 300SL sports racing car, he just knew it had an assured market in North America. Although Daimler-Benz had developed the 300SL strictly as a racer, and had no intention of making it a production car, Max implored the company to do so. To prove that he was serious, he placed an order for 1000 of the sleek machines. This opportunity was too good for D-B to pass up,

Mercedes-Benz 300SL Gullwing.

– BILL VANCE

war designs, the 300 sedan and slightly sportier 300S, in 1951. With production cars well under way, the company set out to recover some of its pre-war racing glory. Mercedes-Benz decided to return to competition using components from the 300 model.

While Mercedes-Benz and its German rival, Auto-Union, had been almost invincible in Grand Prix racing in the 1930s, Mercedes wasn't financially or technically ready to re-enter Formula One competition by the early '50s.

Its plan was to use less rigorous sports car racing as an interim route to full GP participation.

and plans were launched for a production 300SL.

Daimler-Benz had introduced its new post-

127

the driver in entry, the steering wheel could be tilted away from the steering column. Confined parking spaces presented their own special challenge. Once inside, the passengers were snug and comfortable compared with the usual roadster sports car, and enjoyed excellent visibility.

The 2996 cubic centimetre 300 sedan engine was quite modestly stressed in stock form, producing just 115 horsepower at 4600 rpm. Before they were finished with it, the engineers would be pulling out considerably more than 200.

When the production 300SL was introduced to the public, it would be listed at 240 horsepower by the generous Society of Automotive Engineers (SAE) gross rating method. It was a tall engine, and to accommodate it under the 300SL's low hood, the six was tilted over 50 degrees to the left.

Carburetors had been used in the early stages of the 300SL's development, but when the car became a production model, it would be fitted with Bosch fuel injection, the world's first production gasoline-engined car to have this feature. It also had dry-sump lubrication, a practice borrowed from racing.

The 300SL quickly made its mark in competition, winning, among others, the 1952 Le Mans, France, 24-hour endurance race and the Carrera Panamericana (Mexican Road Race). It was also quite successful in rallying.

With its competition credentials well established, the Mercedes-Benz 300SL gullwing

Although the 300 sedan was not adaptable to racing, its driveline and chassis components, including the now maligned swing axles, were heavy, and would prove to be extremely robust. The 3.0-litre, single overhead cam, 12-valve, in-line six had an almost square (equal bore and stroke) design. Its fully counterweighted, forged steel crankshaft ran in seven large main bearings.

For competition, the engineers designed a small, aerodynamic (its coefficient of drag was an ultra-low 0.25) aluminum-bodied coupe. It was called the 300SL (3.0 litre engine, plus Sport and Light). Because the 300 sedan frame was too heavy for a competition car, a "space frame" was used - a bridge-like structure made by welding together many small diameter tubes.

This achieved the goals of strength and lightness, but the space frame also extended halfway up the sides of the car, precluding the use of regular doors. To provide adequate door openings, the designers placed the bottom of the door as high as necessary to clear the structure. They then extended the top of the door into the roof, hinging it near the middle of the reinforced roof. The result was the so-called gullwing doors, the 300SL's most striking and often imitated feature. What, then, had started as the solution to an engineering problem turned into a significant styling trademark.

The gullwing doors made entry and exit tricky, particularly for women wearing skirts. To assist coupe, and its less potent sibling, the four-cylinder 190SL convertible, made their debut at the New York Auto Show in February, 1954. Suddenly everything else in the world looked a little old. The 300SL was a sensation with the public and the motoring press.

In the hands of the testers the 300SL fulfilled its promise. *Road & Track* magazine reported in its April, 1955, issue that the 240 hp, 3.0 litre engine would accelerate the 2710 pound (1230 kg) coupe from 0 to 60 mph (96 km/h) in just 7.4 seconds. It would sprint from 0 to 100 mph (161 km/h) in a mere 17.2 seconds, and reached a two-way top speed average of 134.2 mph (216 km/h), although *R & T* opined that 140 mph (225 km/h) should be possible with a different axle ratio. The testers summed it up as "...the ultimate as an all-round sports car," and said that "The sports car of the future is here today."

As would be expected, the 300SL also had a hefty price - some $8000, a lot of money when a pretty nice Cadillac could be had new for $5000. This, in part, no doubt accounts for the fact that only 1400 gullwing coupes were produced from 1954 to '57, when it was replaced by a roadster. The roadster's frame was modified to allow the use of conventional doors. It would remain in production until 1963, by which time it was getting a little dated. Total production was 1858.

Although built only from 1954 to '57, the Mercedes-Benz 300SL gullwing coupe left an indelible impression on the motoring world. It introduced fuel injection to production gasoline powered cars, a significant first. And its gullwing doors made a styling statement that has rarely been matched. It will always rank among the great automobile designs, and is an almost priceless collectible today.

METROPOLITAN

1954 Metropolitan.

– CHRYSLER CANADA

George Mason was only the second president of the Nash Motor Co., having taken over from the original president Charles Nash in 1937. He became chairman in 1948 when Nash died. He and his successor George Romney were men ahead of their time. Mason foresaw the need for smaller, lighter, more economical and better handling vehicles. And Romney carried on preaching the gospel of the compact car when he became president of American Motors, the company formed through Nash's merger with Hudson in 1954.

Mason brought out the first post-war compact, the Nash Rambler, in 1950. He then combined with Donald Healey of England to develop and market the Nash-Healey sports car. Encouraged by the success of the Rambler, and undaunted by the demise of the little American Bantam in 1941, and the imminent end of the tiny Crosley, Mason wanted to make an even smaller car than the Rambler.

In 1949 he commissioned the construction of a little two-door experimental convertible model based on Fiat mechanical components. It was named the NXI, for Nash Experimental International. In 1950 Mason sent it on a tour of the country to test public opinion. (The underlying question was: Is America ready for the $1000 car?) This was followed by a hard-top version, the NKI (Nash-Kelvinator International).

130

Response was deemed favorable enough to warrant production and the new 2/3 passenger Nash Metropolitan debuted in March, 1954, in hardtop and convertible forms.

The Austin Motor Co. Ltd., Birmingham, England, provided the engine and running gear, and assembled the cars in co-operation with coach builder Fisher & Ludlow who built the unit construction chassis-body. The Metro was powered by a 1200 cc (73.2 cubic inch) overhead valve, Austin A-40 four-cylinder engine, which developed 42 horsepower. This may not sound like much power today, but it outpowered the popular Volkswagen Beetle's 30 horsepower.

Assuming that North American drivers preferred a three-speed transmission, Nash had the Austin A-40 gearbox modified to eliminate first gear. Unfortunately, the synchromesh of the Austin transmission's second gear (which became first in the Metro) was sacrificed in the process, but then, others didn't have a synchro low in those days either. To make domestic drivers feel even more at home the gearshift lever was on the steering column, or more correctly, seemed to almost grow out of the dashboard à la the Nash Rambler.

In spite of its diminutive size - it rode on an 85-inch (2159 mm) wheelbase, and was only 149.5 inches (3797 mm) long - the Metropolitan was quite a stylish little car. It looked for all the world like a large Nash that had been shrunk down to fit an Austin chassis. It still, however, seemed to dwarf its tiny 5.20 x 13 tires and 13-inch wheels, (the VW, although lighter, had 5.60 x 15 tires).

The performance of the baby Nash was good compared with its competition. In a four-car road test published in August, 1954, Road & Track magazine recorded a zero to 60 mph (96 km/h) acceleration time of 22.4 seconds for the Metro, which compared very favorably with the VW's time of 39.2.

It did, however, suffer from the problem that afflicted all small cars of the day (except the VW): a very low drive axle ratio. Thus, while the Beetle's engine was revving at less than 3000 rpm at 60 mph (96 km/h), the poor little Metro's was churning out 4300 rpm.

In 1956 American Motors fitted the Metropolitan with the 1.5 litre 52-horsepower Austin engine for even better performance. It also received a more elaborate mesh-type grille to replace the single bar, and over the years other amenities such as a trunk lid and window vents were added.

After the Nash/Hudson merger, Metros were marketed with both Nash and Hudson badges for a few years, before becoming simply AMC Metropolitans. A few were also sold in England.

A nice example of the Metropolitan is owned by Nancy Gray of Islington, Ontario. She is the third owner (the first was a "little old lady from Cobourg" - honest), of this 1961 hardtop, and she drives it almost every day for shopping and other family errands. A short test drive (pull the choke right out, pull the starter knob) gave several interesting impressions, among them the large steering wheel, heavy brakes, excellent visibility, but most of all, the spirited performance. The little 1.5 litre Austin engine steps right out, especially in high gear. Nancy says it cruises nicely at 65 mph (105 km/h) and is very economical on fuel.

The Metropolitan could be termed only a moderate sales success. But although it didn't achieve anything like the market penetration of the VW Beetle, it was a milestone of sorts by being the first really usable small car from an American manufacturer. It was offered from 1954 to 1962, with 1959 being the best year when 22,209 were built; total production was 94,986. In 1962 a mere 420 were produced.

The Metro was an example of what could be achieved by wedding sturdy British components with contemporary American styling, but in the process it came out as being neither British nor American. And unfortunately it was ahead of its time. But time vindicates many things and the Metropolitan has finally come into its own. Today, according to Mississauga auto appraiser Dean Renwick, it has a dedicated following as a collectible, a statement borne out by the existence of the U.S.-based Metropolitan Owners Club of North America Inc., which, Nancy Gray tells me, has some 3000 members.

MG TD

The English MG name dates back to the early 1920s. That's when Cecil Kimber, manager and race driver with Morris Garages, which made the Morris car, modified a "bull-nosed" Morris and called it an MG, after Morris Garages. Although history is often amorphous, the MG seems to have evolved into a production model in 1924. The first M-type MG Midget, with a pointed tail and fabric body, appeared in 1929 as an adaptation of the overhead cam Morris Minor. It provided sporting motoring at a very reasonable cost.

The marque became highly regarded in England and amassed an enviable racing record in the 1930s, particularly in the 750 cubic centimetre

MG TD.

— BILL VANCE

the years just after World War II.

The first post-World War II MGs to arrive here in the late 1940s were the MG TC Midget models. They were really just slightly modified TA and TB carry-overs from the '30s. Tall wire wheels, rakish clamshell fenders, cut-down doors and a folding windshield made the TC, to quote *Mechanix Illustrated* magazine's pioneer car tester, Tom McCahill, "a debonair little aristocrat." The roadster, he added, "looked sporty, expensive and intriguing as a night on the Orient Express."

But for all of its classical styling the TC was pretty limited in both performance and riding

class. Although a few were imported privately, the MG was little known in North America until

133

qualities. A front suspension consisting of a solid beam axle and stiff leaf springs were combined with the skittishness of ultra-quick steering (1.7 turns lock to lock).

That made the TC a handful to drive at its modest 75 mph - plus (121 km/h) top speed on anything but a surface of billiard table smoothness. Even though they came here in small numbers and with only right-hand drive, the little MG TC introduced North Americans to the charm of the English sports car. And in so doing it brought a whole new element of fun to driving.

Such an archaic design could not endure for long, however, and in late 1949 TC production ceased, and the works in Abingdon-on-Thames began turning out the more modern TD model. In spite of howls of protest from the purists who decried the "Hollywoodizing" of the MG, the TD was a far better car.

It had independent double-wishbone-and-coil-spring front suspension derived from the MG Y-Series sedan, and was guided by the superior rack and pinion steering. In place of the tall, spidery 19-inch wire wheels with knock-off hubs, which admittedly had their own special attraction, were 15-inch pressed steel bolt-on types. They weren't nearly as aesthetically "pure," but they were stronger, less expensive and maintenance-free.

Although "softer" in appearance, the TD retained the over-all "square" configuration and styling features of the TC, including the clamshell fenders, folding windshield and cut-down doors hinged at the rear. A wider body provided more interior space, and the tacho-meter and speedometer were now together in front of the driver, rather than having the speedo away over on the passenger's side as the TC did. And left-hand drive was fitted to models exported to countries requiring it.

The driveline, a 1250 cc (76.3 cubic inch), 54-horsepower, overhead valve inline four mated to a four-speed manual transmission, was carried over into the TD. It wasn't much power to motivate a 2000-pound (907 kg) car, so in terms of raw performance the TD was not very fast when compared with such American cars as Olds 88s or Fords.

In 1952 Tom McCahill of *Mechanix Illustrated* took his own MG Mark II, which he dubbed "McGillicuddy the Mighty," to the sands of Daytona Beach, Florida for the annual Speed Week event held there in February by the National Association for Stock Car Auto Racing. In spite of a strong wind he managed a two-way average of 79.49 mph (128 km/h), which he claimed was a new top speed record for stock cars in Class F (1100 to 1500 cc engine displacement).

Road & Track magazine ran a comparison test between the TD and the 60-horsepower TD Mark II in its February 1953 issue. The Mark II had a "factory hop-up" which included such items as higher compression, larger carburetors and valves, stiffer valve springs, two fuel pumps, eight shock absorbers rather than four, and a higher (4.875:1 vs. 5.125:1) rear axle ratio. They recorded a 0-to-60 mph (96 km/h) acceleration time of 19.4 for the TD and 16.5 for the Mark II. Top speed averages were 78.9 and 81.25 mph (127 and 131 km/h) respectively. This is probably a fair representation of the performance difference between the two models.

MG speeds, then, were definitely not in the Jaguar class. But raw performance numbers were not what the MG was about. It was the quintessential sports car and its forté was nimble handling, fast cornering, and just plain driving enjoyment. With those cut-down doors and wind-in-the-face driving, they at least felt fast. Owners raced and rallied them, joined sports car clubs and enjoyed a kind of esoteric camaraderie that eluded ordinary motorist "Joe Practical," as McCahill called him, as he sedately commuted to and from work in his Plymouth or Chevy.

The MG TD continued through 1953 when it was replaced by the TF, a transitional model that would bridge the gap between the square T-Series cars and the envelope-bodied MGA of 1956. By this time, the TD had been surpassed in performance and styling by such cars as the Triumph TR2 and Austin-Healey 100.

Over its four-year life span, almost 30,000 MG TDs were built, of which approximately 75 per

cent were exported to North America. In spite of its modest performance, it brought a new *joie de vivre* to driving over here.

The TD's place in automotive history is secure because it, more than any other vehicle, laid the foundation for the sports car movement in the U.S. and Canada. Not surprisingly, those early MGs are favorite collectibles today. Few marques have a more enthusiastic following than those who love, preserve and enjoy driving their T-Series MGs.

NASH-HEALEY

1953 Nash-Healey.

– RICHARD SPIEGELMAN

Sports car interest in North America was ignited in the late 1940s and early '50s by the appearance of such cars as the English MG TC, and the later TD, the Jaguar XK120 and the Austin-Healey. American automakers then responded with their Kaiser-Darrins, Chevrolet Corvettes and Ford Thunderbirds.

An astute automobile man who sensed the rising sports car interest early was George Mason, chairman of Nash Motor Co. of Kenosha, Wisc. Mason had gone to Europe in 1949 and become enamored with the sports cars he saw there. This led to thoughts of jazzing up the stodgy Nash image, and while returning to America he encountered English sports car builder Donald Healey aboard the ocean liner Queen Elizabeth. It surely seemed like fate.

Healey, a motor racer and practical engineer, had succeeded in establishing his own company, the Donald Healey Motor Co. Ltd., in Warwick, just after World War II. It produced several models, one of the best known being the Silverstone, which was powered by a 2.4 litre Riley overhead-valve four.

Healey liked big engines, however, and one of his interests was in producing a car with an English chassis and a large American engine, as had been done by others such as the Hudson-powered Railton and the Ford V-8 powered Jensen. In fact the purpose of the U.S. trip was to see whether he could purchase a supply of Cadillac's new short-stroke, overhead valve V-8s.

Being car men their discussion naturally turned to their plans. When Healey revealed the reason for his journey, Mason was quick to assure him that if Cadillac couldn't supply engines, Nash certainly could. When Healey subsequently learned that Cadillac needed all the V-8s it could produce, he turned to Mason, and that's how the Nash-Healey was born.

A few Nash Ambassador overhead valve in-line six engines and drivelines were soon on their way to England. Healey's craftsmen got to work immediately and had a prototype two-seater Nash-Healey ready in time for the 1950 Le Mans, France, 24-hour endurance race.

To the surprise of everyone, the overdrive-equipped (the first overdrive at Le Mans) Nash-Healey finished fourth in a formidable 66-car field, beaten only by two Talbots and an Allard. It was an auspicious start for a new car; and to prove that it wasn't beginner's luck, Nash-Healeys would finish sixth in 1951 and third in '52.

Encouraged by the initial Le Mans success, Mason and Healey plunged ahead with a Nash-Healey production car. An attractive envelope-type, two-seater roadster body was designed, and the Panelcraft body works of Birmingham was contracted to produce them in aluminum.

A Nash grille, bumpers and other body parts were used, and the Healey engineers modified the

234.8 cubic inch (3.8 litre) Nash engine with such items as a higher-compression aluminum head, a hotter camshaft, and two English SU carburetors, raising the horsepower from 112 to 125.

The Nash driveline was fitted, and the front suspension was the somewhat unusual single trailing arm type that Healey had used on his Silverstone model. At the rear could be found a solid axle and coil springs. The car was trim, with a 102 inch (2591 mm) wheelbase and an over-all length of 170 inches (4318 mm). The aluminum body held weight down to a reasonable 2700 pounds (1225 kg).

Nash-Healey production got under way late in 1950 and it made its European debut at the 1950 London and Paris Motor Shows. It was shown to North America at the Chicago Motor Show in February, 1951. As the first post-war American sports car from an established manufacturer, except for the tiny Crosley Hotshot, it created quite a sensation.

With the big Nash engine in a relatively light car, the Nash-Healey offered good performance. According to Tom McCahill of Mechanix Illustrated magazine, it could accelerate from 0 to 60 mph (96 km/h) in 11.5 seconds, and reach a top speed of 106 mph (171 km/h). This was, however, far off the pace of the rival Jaguar XK120, which could do 0 to 60 (96) in 10 seconds, and top 120 (193).

As far as handling was concerned, McCahill's

assessment was delivered with his usual flamboyance. "I want to go on record right now," he wrote, "and say I have never driven a sports car that handled better or gave the driver so much control in a power-glide or spin."

The Nash-Healey, then, came with a lot of promise. It had good handling, pleasant styling, race-proven performance, and a sturdy American drivetrain. All of this should have added up to strong sales, but it didn't. The problem was the price.

Shipping the drivetrain to Britain, assembling the car, and then shipping it back to North America was expensive. The result was that the N-H carried a price in the $4000 range, the same as the Jaguar XK120. In the eyes of most buyers the Nash-Healey was weak tea beside the power, performance and styling of the Jag. Only slightly over 100 of the '51s were sold.

Nash engaged famed Italian designer Pinin Farina to restyle its full-size Nashes for 1952 and he also turned his hand to the Nash-Healey. The new styling, and larger 252.6 cubic inch (4.1 litre) 140 hp engine that was phased in during 1952, should have helped sales.

Unfortunately, since Pinin Farina was now building the bodies - now of steel - a trip to Italy was added to the cost. This resulted in a price close to $6000, which was too rich for most buyers. Only 150 '52s would be sold. Nash would carry on with the Nash-Healey for a couple of more years, adding a stylish Le Mans coupe in '53.

By the time production stopped in 1954 and the Nash-Healey slipped into history, a total of 506 had been built. It had been a valiant attempt by an American manufacturer to pioneer something different and exciting, but the method of execution proved too expensive.

NASH RAMBLER

The Rambler name goes back almost to the dawn of the century. It was in 1902 that former bicycle builder Thomas B. Jeffrey began manufacturing a little one-cylinder car in Kenosha, Wis. He called it the Rambler, the same name he had applied to his bicycles. The subject of this story is a much more modern version of the Rambler, but it had, nevertheless, a direct connection to that first Rambler car.

It was a classic rags-to-riches story in which Charles Nash rose from abandoned child at age six in 1870, to the presidency of General Motors in 1912. But Nash resigned from GM in 1916 after a clash with founder Billy Durant who had regained control of the corporation. Nash then

1951 Nash Rambler.

– RICHARD SHEGELMAN

bought the Thomas B. Jeffrey Co., which was by then calling its cars Jeffreys, not Ramblers. He changed it to Nash Motors Co. and the cars became Nashes.

In spite of some ups and downs, the Nash company prospered over the years and developed a solid reputation. It amalgamated with refrigerator maker Kelvinator in 1937 to become the Nash-Kelvinator Corp., and brought full unit-body car construction to the American scene with the new Nash 600 (600 miles from a 20-gallon tank of fuel) in 1941.

After World War II, during which Nash manufactured such items as aircraft engines and parts, the company returned to producing pre-

139

war designs until it could come up with its more modern "Airflyte" model in 1949.

In 1950 Nash revived the Rambler name in "America's first compact car." Although GM and Ford had considered building smaller cars right after the war, they had abandoned the idea. It fell to independent Nash to make the leap. The Crosley was on the scene too, but it was too small to be practical.

Compared with standard size cars of the day, the Rambler was indeed compact. Whereas the Chevrolet, for example, had a wheelbase of 115 inches (2921 mm) and weighed some 3200 pounds (1452 kg), the diminutive new Nash rode on a wheelbase of only 100 inches (2540 mm) and tipped the scales at a mere 2420 pounds (1098 kg).

Like its larger siblings, the Rambler had unit construction and a smaller version of the corporations's bulbous "inverted bathtub" design. On the smaller car, however, it seemed to come off better.

It was introduced first as a stylish convertible, but with the unusual feature of having the side window frames fixed in place. This allowed the top to be pulled up along these rails something like a window blind by an electric motor and a system of cables. A station wagon soon followed, and the Rambler was rounded out in later years to include a full line of body styles.

Power came from a 172.6 cubic inch (2.8 litre) side-valve six-cylinder engine that developed 82 horsepower, and was also used in the larger Statesman model, which had replaced the 600. While not a tire burner, it provided reasonable performance and excellent economy. Tom McCahill, *Mechanix Illustrated* magazine's car tester, estimated that the Rambler might get up to 35 miles per U.S. gallon, although 30 would probably have been more realistic.

Through a stroke of luck and a little old-fashioned horse trading, McCahill scooped the media and got the Rambler onto the cover of the May, 1950, issue of *Mechanix Illustrated*. How he achieved this, and got to be the first journalist to drive the baby Nash, is an interesting little anecdote.

Arriving ahead of schedule at Nash's Burlington, Wis., proving ground to test a Nash Ambassador in the fall of 1949, Tom inadvertently stumbled onto a fleet of Ramblers that were being tested by company engineers.

Once he had seen them, of course, the cat was out of the bag. A deal was made, and in exchange for a promise to keep the lid on the story until the official spring introduction date of the new car, "Uncle Tom McBlackmail" was allowed to test drive it several months before it made its public debut.

Although he didn't have an opportunity to conduct a full road test, Tom was able to determine that the little Rambler had a top speed of

84 to 86 mph (135 to 138 km/h), and that it had "excellent riding qualities and quite a bit of snap and punch."

The Rambler turned out to be the most successful of the early post-World War II American compacts. These included the Henry J from Kaiser-Frazer (and a rebadged version called the Allstate from Sears, Roebuck and Co.), the Aero Willys from Willys-Overland, and the Hudson Jet from Hudson.

Some 26,000 Ramblers were produced during the first model year, which was really less than half a year. In 1951, 80,000 were built, a remarkable achievement for a new model from a relatively small company. For 1953, the Rambler received the Pinin Farina styling that characterized all Nashes at that time, and began the inevitable American car growth cycle by having its wheelbase stretched to 108 inches (2743 mm) in the sedan model.

Nash joined Hudson to form American Motors Corp. in 1954 and production of the original Rambler was discontinued in 1955, although larger cars bearing the Rambler name were produced.

Sensing a return to smaller cars, AMC resurrected the 100-inch (2540 mm) wheelbase Rambler for 1958, and renamed it the American. It went on to become the Hornet in 1970, later the Concord, and even later the four-wheel drive AMC Eagle.

The Rambler, as well as being the first and most successful of the early post-WW II compact cars, figured very significantly in American Motors history. It helped Nash through a difficult time before its merger with Hudson. Later the Rambler, along with Jeep which AMC acquired in 1970, and some help from Renault of France, saved the corporation. AMC disappeared as an entity when it was bought by Chrysler in 1987 and became its Jeep-Eagle Division.

The original 1950 Rambler is fondly remembered by many. It was attractive (McCahill said it was "as cute as a cupcake") and reliable, and deserves its place in automotive history. It was a pioneering effort to produce a sensibly sized, economical family car, the car that became synonymous with the term "compact." That's not a bad legacy for a car that was named after a bicycle.

OLDSMOBILE – CURVED DASH

Over the years, cars have been the inspiration for several songs, an art form that seemed to reach its peak in the late '50s and early '60s. There was "Little GTO" (for the Pontiac GTO, the first muscle car), by Ronny And The Daytonas (their big hit). "Little Deuce Coupe" (1932 Ford) came from the Beach Boys, who also did a song in honor of an engine, "409" (for the 409 cubic inch Chevrolet V-8). Probably the earliest car-inspired song was "In My Merry Oldsmobile," written in 1905 by Gus Edwards and Vincent Bryan and dedicated to the Curved Dash Oldsmobile.

Ransom Eli Olds had been experimenting with cars since the 1880s and succeeded in

1905 Curved Dash Oldsmobile.

– BILL VANCE

building his first one, a three-wheeled steamer in 1887, and then another steam powered vehicle in 1891. Olds became disenchanted with steam and turned out his first gas-powered car in 1896. He made several more and in 1897 he organized the Olds Motor Vehicle Co., in Lansing, Mich.

Like so many fledging automakers of the day, Olds ran into cash flow difficulties and by mid-1898 only five or six cars had been built. Financial assistance came from Samuel L. Smith, a lumber magnate and millionaire, and the company relocated to Detroit.

Smith's two sons were graduating from college and dad was looking for a business for them to participate in. In the spring of 1899, the assets of the old firm plus some new money from Smith were used to organize the Olds Motor Works.

With the financial worries out of the way, Olds set to work designing several new cars. These were to be brought to market in 1901, although there was some concern about the number of different models Olds was developing.

At this point there occurred one of those ironic twists of fate that seem to happen so often in automotive history. In the spring of 1901 the Olds plant was destroyed by fire. During the blaze, the only thing that workers were able to save was a prototype of a curved dash runabout which they pushed out of the burning building. There was no problem now with too many models; the direction of the Olds Motor Works was set because they had only one. Oldsmobile continued in Detroit for a few years, and then in 1904 relocated back to Lansing, its original home.

The Curved Dash Oldsmobile was a jaunty little car with its dashboard that curled up in front of the driver and passenger in a gentle flowing arc. Its 95.4 cubic inch (1.6 litre) single-cylinder engine developed seven horsepower at 500 rpm, causing wags to say it made "one chug per telegraph pole." It was located under the seat and drove the rear wheels through a two-speed transmission and chain drive. Steering was by a tiller, and those seven horsepower could propel the 700-pound (318 kg) car to almost 25 mph

(40 km/h). It was a model of simplicity. The longitudinal leaf springs on each side of the vehicle, for example, also acted as the frame.

But speed wasn't as important as reliability in those early days, and here the little Oldsmobile excelled. Olds bought his engines from the Leland and Falconer machine shop in Detroit, the best engine builders in Michigan, and probably in all of America.

Oldsmobile was able to rebuild the plant and assemble 425 cars in 1901, a remarkable achievement. The Curved Dash Oldsmobile was strongly promoted with advertising, and by demonstrations at such events as fairs. This, backed up by several successful long-distance endurance runs, got sales off to a brisk start.

The little car proved itself sound, and production rose to 2500 in 1902, 4000 in 1903, and 5508 in 1904. Oldsmobile, therefore, became the first mass-produced car in America.

At this point, Olds and the Smith brothers had an irreconcilable difference of opinion. He wanted to continue selling light, affordable cars, particularly his beloved Curved Dash, while the Smiths preferred heavier, more expensive vehicles. Olds lost the argument and left the company.

Several months later the indomitable Olds had formed another auto firm, the R. E. Olds Co. The Smiths immediately began jumping all over him, threatening lawsuits, and charging him with infringement on the rights to his name, which he had sold.

Olds paused, reconsidered, and concluded that if he had sold his name, he hadn't sold his initials. He then went ahead and became the Reo Motor Car Co.

Oldsmobile produced 6500 cars in 1905, the year in which Edwards and Bryan wrote their song. By 1906, however, whether because of the loss of Olds's expertise, or whether the market was not ready for heavier Oldsmobiles - the Smith's had relegated the Curved Dash to a minor place in their lineup - production fell to just 1600 cars.

By 1907, the year in which Curved Dash production ceased, the total number of Oldsmobiles built was down to 1200. In 1908 production declined to 1055 and the financially stressed company fell into the arms of Billy Durant's newly organized General Motors Co. There it survived, then thrived, and went on to become North America's oldest continuous automobile manufacturer. Although Durant had made many ill advised purchases during his periods with General Motors, Oldsmobile would not prove to be one of them.

Regardless of the strength of the Olds Motor Works, by 1908 the Curved Dash Oldsmobile's time had passed anyway. It was too small and light to compete with the larger cars coming on the market, especially models like Henry Ford's Model T. It had, however, filled an important niche in the early years, and proved its popularity by becoming America's first mass produced car, not to mention the inspiration for a song.

OLDSMOBILE "ROCKET" 88

The 1949 Oldsmobile "Rocket" 88 could be called the 1932 Ford of its day. Just as Henry Ford had installed a powerful V-8 engine in a light body back in 1932 and created one of the most spirited cars on the road, Oldsmobile followed the same recipe in 1949 with the same results. While each was the performance sensation of its day, the Rocket 88 moved it to a higher plateau, and really began the modern era of high performance cars.

Both were pioneering efforts under the hood. Whereas Ford had brought smooth, velvety V-8 power to the popularly priced field, Oldsmobile - along with Cadillac - introduced the short stroke, high compression, overhead valve V-8 to the

1949 Oldsmobile "Rocket" 88.

— GENERAL MOTORS

world. It was the type of powerplant that would be the staple of the North American auto industry for some 30 years, and it still has an important place to this day.

This would not be the first V-8 for Oldsmobile. It had had one for a few years beginning in 1915, and its short-lived Viking "companion" car of 1929-30 was also fitted with a V-8. The Viking was supposed to be a kind of lower priced La Salle, Cadillac's recently introduced marque, but the beginning of the Depression quickly killed it.

Oldsmobile began working on its new V-8, which it called the Rocket, in 1946. The engine was based on experimental work done by GM research director Charles Kettering. Kettering layout because its short crankshaft was sturdier than that of an in-line six or eight, and also because it was a more compact design.

Cadillac was also working on a new overhead valve, short stroke, high compression V-8, which was introduced in 1949, but the new Olds and Caddy engines shared no common parts.

The Olds V-8 Rocket engine appeared in the fall of 1948 in Oldsmobile's top-of-the-line 98 series. It displaced 303.7 cubic inches (5.0 litres), developed 135 horsepower, and replaced the 257 cubic inch (4.2 litre) 115 horsepower side-valve, inline eight which dated back to 1932. The 76 series continued with Oldsmobile's side-valve, inline six.

Although the 98, which along with the smaller model Cadillacs had received its new post-war "Futuramic" styling in 1948, was well received, the Olds engineers had an even better trick up their sleeves. After receiving somewhat reluctant corporate approval, they slipped their new V-8 into the light 76 series, new-for-1949 A-body, which was also shared with Chevrolet and Pontiac. The Olds division designated the new series the 88 to slot it between the 76 and the 98. The Oldsmobile 88 series was introduced as a mid-year model in February 1949, instantly becoming know as the Rocket 88.

The new 88, even though it was only a half-year model, helped substantially increase Olds-mobile's sales form 171,518 in 1948 to 288,310 in

was a brilliant engineer who counted among his many accomplishments the invention of the electric self-starter for the 1912 Cadillac, a true watershed in automotive history, and the condenser ignition system. Kettering's earlier work, along with co-worker Thomas Midgley, an engineer and chemist, in which they studied the problem of engine combustion knock, really made the high compression engine possible. Their experiments led them to the idea of adding tetraethyl lead to gasoline. This raised the octane, or resistance to knock, of the fuel, which allowed the use of much higher compression ratios. This "ethyl" gasoline, as it was called, went on sale in the mid-20s.

Though compression ratios were gradually rising, Kettering was convinced that the potential had not been nearly fully exploited. Just after World War II he built an experimental six-cylinder engine with the unheard of compression ratio of 12.0:1. He proved that it could deliver 35 to 40 percent better fuel economy, and develop 25 percent more power than the normal 6.25:1 ratio. When he delivered a paper on his work in high compression to the Society of Automotive Engineers in 1947, he started a revolution in thinking among Detroit's automakers.

Oldsmobile engineers were very enthusiastic about Kettering's findings and quickly pressed forward with the development of their high compression engine. They settled on the V-8 the 1949 model year. In 1950 Olds sales reached 407,289, of which 268,414 were 88s. The success of the 88 convinced Olds to discontinue the six-cylinder 76 series.

While it was doing well in the showrooms, the new 88 was also cleaning up on the tracks. Overnight the Rocket 88 vaulted Oldsmobile from a somewhat staid, conservative car to a ripsnorting high performance machine that soon became a frequent winner on the National Association for Stock Car Auto Racing (NASCAR) circuits. It won six of the nine NASCAR late-model division races in 1949, 10 of 19 in 1950 and 20 of 41 in 1952. Although Oldsmobile's racing glory would be superseded by the low-slung Hudson Hornet with its powerful six-cylinder engine, it was still the first real "King of NASCAR."

For 1951 Olds had introduced the Super 88 based on the heavier GM B-body, also used by Buick, and although the A-body 88 was continued, the division began concentrating its sales efforts on the larger model. By the mid-50s, everybody was in the V-8 game. Chrysler had brought out its fabulous V-8 Hemi in 1951, and Ford and other GM divisions had overhead valve V-8s too.

But the Oldsmobile Rocket engine had built up a lasting reputation. In the 1970s, about a quarter century after the original Rocket appeared, GM moved to a corporate engine policy

so it could mix and match its powerplant offerings through various car lines. The result was that some Oldsmobile owners, much to their surprise, found Chevrolet V-8s under their hoods. Even though the Chevy engine was a later and more sophisticated design which had proved its power and durability in countless forms of competition, owners were so soundly convinced of the Rocket engine's superiority, and were so incensed, that they took GM to court for misrepresenting its product.

The matter was eventually resolved, but it was a demonstration of the strength of the reputation that the Oldsmobile Rocket 88 engine had built up. It was truly one of the benchmarks in American automotive engineering; few other automobile engines in history have established such a powerful image.

OLDSMOBILE TORONADO

1966 Oldsmobile Toronado.

– GENERAL MOTORS

Front-wheel drive is now the most popular way of getting the power to the road in passenger cars, but its widespread use is a relatively recent development. It was only during the 1980s that the domestic industry made the transition in a big way, although there had been significant pioneering work done in both Europe and America.

Alvis of England and Tracta of France had introduced production front-wheel drive cars in the late '20s. This was followed by Audi of Germany in 1931 with its truly advanced Front model, which forecast most of our present layouts with its transverse engine, front-wheel drive and four-wheel independent suspension. The car that would do the most to popularize front-wheel drive was the French Citroen Traction Avant, which came out in 1934 and lasted right through to the '50s.

On this side of the Atlantic, the Christie Front Drive Motor Co. had front-wheel drive racers running as early as 1904, with production models available by 1905. Ruxton and Gardner also tried fwd but soon gave up. Harry Miller had used front-wheel drive very successfully in his dominant Indianapolis racers in the 1920s and '30s. But by far the best known American front drive car was the Cord, the first of which was the 1929 L-29 model.

Although front drive continued to be used in Europe, it languished in North America. It was

148

revived in 1966 by GM's innovative Oldsmobile division in the Toronado, to be followed a year later by Cadillac's Eldorado coupe.

General Motors had introduced some imaginative engineering in the 1960s, including the rear-engined Chevrolet Corvair, the Pontiac Tempest's "hanging rope" driveshaft connected to a rear-mounted transaxle, and passenger car turbocharging in the Olds F-85 Jetfire V-8 and Corvair Monza Spyder.

But the item that would have the greatest long-term impact on GM's future was the front-wheel drive which debuted in those '60s Oldsmobiles and Cadillacs. The use of front-wheel drive had been considered by GM during and right after World War II when it was looking into producing a smaller car. Then in the early '50s it was tried again for its LaSalle II Motorama concept car, but was abandoned because of time and cost considerations.

The idea was revived in the late '50s and promoted by the bright young Olds engineer, John Beltz, who would go on to become general manager of Oldsmobile. Oldsmobile was a good place to suggest this because it already had a proud reputation for innovative engineering, having pioneered the fully automatic hydraulic "Hydra-Matic" transmission in 1940, and, along with Cadillac, the overhead valve, short-stroke V-8 engine in 1949. Oldsmobile wanted a specialty car to compete

149

with the successful Riviera from its Buick sister division, and the very popular Ford Thunderbird. But Beltz wanted something different, something with a little engineering pizzazz. He rallied his colleagues, and soon convinced the corporation to let Oldsmobile build a front-drive car.

The front-wheel drive Toronado that emerged in 1966 was a sensation. With a wheelbase of 119 inches (3023 mm), an overall length of 211 inches (5359 mm), and a weight of 4500 pounds (2042 kg), the Toro was a big car. There were sceptics who predicted that fwd wouldn't be successful on such a large vehicle.

To power this much car required a substantial engine, and Olds provided it in the form of a 425 cubic inch (7.0 litre) overhead valve V-8 rated at 385 horsepower. It was mounted in the normal longitudinal position with the torque converter in its usual location at the rear of the engine.

The three-speed Hydra-Matic, however, was "folded" around 180 degrees and mounted on the left side of the engine. Drive was transmitted from the converter to the transmission via a two-inch (51 mm) wide multi-link chain, which resembled a large timing chain.

Because the drive axles passed through where the front coil springs would normally be located, Oldsmobile used longitudinal torsion bars as the springing medium. Rear suspension was also novel, and simple, in that the beam axle was mounted on a single leaf spring on each side.

But what prospective Toronado buyers were most impressed with first was the virtually flat floor. Eliminating the transmission hump and driveshaft tunnel had allowed Oldsmobile to build a true six-passenger car.

The styling of the Toro was almost as dramatic as the engineering. It had a long nose, and the front end was made to appear even longer by fenders that stretched out ahead of the hood, no doubt to emphasize the front-wheel drive feature.

Hidden headlamps, which had been pioneered by the fwd Cord 810 in 1936, were also fitted. Substantial fender flares front and rear gave the Toro an aggressive look, and the short, sloped fastback body ended in an abrupt vertical chop, following the precept laid down by German aerodynamicist Wunibald Kamm.

The Toronado, the first American front-driver in 30 years, was well received by the motoring press and the public when it debuted as a 1966 model in the fall of '65. *Motor Trend* made it their Car of the Year, and Car Life magazine gave it their Engineering Excellence award.

Almost 41,000 '66 Toronados were sold, which would turn out to be the best sales year of the first generation Toro, which lasted until 1970. Cadillac came on board in 1967 with its front-wheel drive Eldorado, and the corporate twins remained GM's front-drive flagships until the introduction of the 1980 X-cars.

The Toro/Eldo provided GM with a reservoir of engineering experience, and the confidence that would prove invaluable in their almost universal transformation to front-wheel drive in the '80s. By the time they launched their compact fwd X-cars (Chevrolet Citation, Pontiac Phoenix et al.) in mid-1979 they had almost 20 years of planning, designing and producing front-drivers.

PACKARD CARIBBEAN

In the early third of the century Packard was one of the grand old names in automobiles.

Almost from the beginning, when the Packard brothers, J.W. and W.D. of Warren, Ohio, brought out their first single-cylinder model in 1899, the marque would develop a reputation for quality and reliability.

It gradually moved up the social scale to become, along with Peerless and Pierce-Arrow, one of the great "Three Ps" of the luxury car market. And it startled the automotive world with the introduction of its "Twin-Six" V-12 for 1916. Of the Three Ps, only Packard would survive the 1930s.

As it did with others, the Great Depression took its toll on Packard, forcing the company to

1954 Packard Caribbean.

— BILL VANCE

move into the medium priced field with the Light 8 of 1932, and the One-Twenty (for its 120-inch wheelbase) model in 1935. It would, however, manage to hang onto some of its fading prestige by offering a V-12 until 1939.

After World War II, Packard, like others, offered warmed over pre-war designs until it could style a new model. This came in late 1947 and helped Packard do surprisingly well for a couple of years, but in 1949 a decline set in. This was due to a somewhat stodgy image, stronger competition from other new models, and the satisfying of the pent-up demand for cars that had been created by the Depression and the cessation of auto production during the war years.

151

Cadillac had brought out its restyled post-war model in 1948 with what would prove to be trendy new tail fins. This was followed in 1949 by its sensational new short-stroke, overhead valve V-8 engine. Chrysler brought forth new models in 1949, as did Lincoln.

And under the hood, Chrysler would launch its soon-to-be-famous "Hemi" V-8 in 1951, while Lincoln got its overhead valve V-8 in 1952. Packard, because of its limited corporate re-sources, would have to soldier on with an outdated side-valve straight-eight until 1955. Something was clearly needed to rejuvenate the old-time Packard image and recapture some of the old-time prestige. That something came in 1953 in the form of the Packard Caribbean model.

Packard had been experimenting with sporty concept models for a few years, which culminated in a 1952 concept car called the Pan American. It proved very popular on the show circuit, and was the inspiration for the Caribbean.

The Caribbean "sports car" was based on Packard's regular convertible, and thus shared the same 122-inch (3099 mm) wheelbase and most of its sheetmetal. There were, however, some significant styling and luxury items.

The interior was trimmed in leather, and there were many effective exterior touches wrought by Packard stylist Dick Teague, who was quickly proving himself the master of the low-priced restyling. It was a skill that would serve him well in his later role as American Motors' stylist.

The wire-spoke wheels were nicely accented by the full wheel cutouts with chrome surrounds. A hood scoop added character to the front end, while a Continental spare tire finished off the rear.

Power for the Caribbean came from Packard's 327 cubic inch (5.4 litre) side-valve, in-line eight which developed 180 horsepower and was available with Packard's "Ultramatic" automatic transmission.

In spite of being up against three new specialty cars from General Motors, the Cadillac Eldorado, Buick Skylark, and Oldsmobile Fiesta, its 750 sales figure was quite respectable. It was second only to the Skylark's 1690, and well ahead of the Eldorado's 532 and the Fiesta's 458.

Because Packard was really starting to feel the financial pinch brought on by the relentless competition of the big three - GM, Ford and Chrysler - the hoped for V-8 engine and model makeover just couldn't be managed for 1954.

The result was that the Caribbean style was largely carryover, although Teague did dress it up with some two-tone paint schemes and chrome accent strips. And he tried to make it look longer by eliminating the fully cut-out rear wheel openings.

There were, however, changes under the hood. Even though the V-8 wasn't ready yet, Packard did give the Caribbean more power in the form of the corporation's largest engine, a 359 cubic inch (5.9 litre), nine-main-bearing straight-eight that pumped out 212 horsepower, the highest powered post-World War II in-line eight. It was a valiant try, but the 1954 Caribbean attracted only 400 buyers.

As the year drew to a close a significant event occurred for Packard in the boardroom. On Oct. 1st, after months of negotiation, Packard and Studebaker merged to form the Studebaker-Packard Corp. It was a clue to the failing strength of both companies.

For 1955 Teague did a masterful job with a major facelifting. He used all of the contemporary styling clichés, including a wraparound windshield, dummy scoops on the hood and the leading edges of the rear fender, a heavy eggcrate grille, and twin rear fender antennas. He then topped it off with a garish three-tone paint job on the Caribbean.

Under the jukebox exterior the engineers had finally provided a new overhead valve V-8 displacing 352 cubic inches (5.8 litres) and developing 275 horsepower. There was also Packard's new "Torsion Level" torsion bar suspension that was interconnected front-to-rear. The automatic transmission was redesigned, becoming the "Twin-Ultramatic," with shift selections being made on a push-button panel in the middle of the instrument panel.

Although the Buick and Olds specialty models

were gone, a new competitor, the Chrysler 300, joined the Cadillac Eldorado. Studebaker-Packard could only manage to sell 500 of its restyled Caribbeans. When just 276 found buyers in 1956, the Packard Caribbean went into the history books, along with all the other real Packards. It had been a brave attempt at reviving the magic of a once-grand name, but unfortunately it would prove to be too little too late.

PLYMOUTH SUBURBAN 1949

1949 Plymouth Suburan.

— CHRYSLER CORP.

Station wagons hold good memories for a lot of people. Although now being supplanted by mini-vans, the station wagon was for many decades the quintessential family vehicle. Whether loaded with camping gear for a cross-country excursion, or hauling furniture to the cottage, the wagon was a faithful workhorse. Hockey sticks, picnics, Cubs and Brownies, fertilizer, antique treasures, all at one time or another found their way into the back of a station wagon.

The station wagon is nostalgic for another reason too; it traces its heritage back to the magic memories of train travel because it was from the railway station that the station wagon got its name. In order to have room for passengers and their luggage when they were met at the railway station, hotels had car or truck chassis fitted with box-like wooden bodies for extra carrying capacity. Thus the depot hack, later the station wagon, was born.

Prior to World War II, and for a few years after, station wagon bodies had traditionally been constructed out of wood. This made them expensive to build initially, and also to maintain later as they were subject to such maladies as loosening, peeling and rotting. Some of the same upkeep precautions had to be taken with wagons as had to be lavished on classic wooden boats to keep them in good condition.

154

This all changed in 1949 with the introduction of the all-steel station wagon. And the Plymouth Suburban (there would be a Dodge version too) 2-door wagon, part of Chrysler Corp.'s completely restyled post-war line of cars, exemplified the genre. Willys-Overland had actually been first with an all-steel wagon in 1946, but it was more of a utility vehicle based on the rugged Jeep chassis, rather than a comfortable family mover. And away back in 1935 General Motors had brought out its Chevrolet Suburban Carryall, a station wagon of sorts, but in reality just a panel truck with windows and seats.

The 1949 Plymouth Suburban was a true car-like vehicle that combined the ride and convenience features of a sedan with the expanded carrying capacity of a wagon. Its shorter Deluxe model 111-inch (2819 mm) wheelbase chassis made it a fairly compact package. Power came from the usual reliable but unexciting 217.8 cubic inch (3.6 litre) Plymouth side-valve, six cylinder engine that developed 97 horsepower. With a weight of over 3100 pounds (1406 kg), however, the Suburban was not about to break any land speed records.

Tom McCahill of *Mechanix Illustrated* magazine tested one of the first Suburbans. They all came originally in "horse's hoof brown," as he called it, which he went on to say "had all the merchandising appeal that a barrel of raw oysters has for your seasick Aunt Sadie." They were soon made

available in a variety of colors.

Tom said he pounded the Suburban over the road on a trip from New York to Florida and back at 75 to 80 mph (121-129 km/h) and reported that the engine showed no signs of strain or over-heating. It did, however, burn a quart (approximately one litre) of oil every 300 miles (480 km). At normal speeds he reported that the oil consumption returned to zero.

Driving at that speed may not seem like an impressive feat today, but one must remember that this was over 40 years ago. Automotive engineering, metallurgy and oil chemistry, not to mention highway engineering, have all come a long way since then.

McCahill also praised the comfort and handling of the Suburban. One of the things that really impressed him was its un-station wagon-like qualities of quietness, and the lack of squeaks and rattles. "The Suburban was as quiet as a bought-off insurance witness," said Tom. With its vinyl interior and fold-down rear seat that formed a flat loading platform, it was also a very utilitarian package.

One of the things that didn't thrill him was the traditional Chrysler sensitivity to dampness, although he did test it in a somewhat severe way – by driving it in the Atlantic Ocean. When a particularly large wave shorted out the ignition Tom was lucky to get the Plymouth out of the water using the starter motor. If he hadn't, the wagon would have gradually sunk into the sand, and Tom would have had some explaining to do to the Chrysler Corporation.

As would be expected, the Suburban was no performance ball of fire; McCahill reported a very leisurely zero to 60 mph (96 km/h) acceleration time of 24.6 seconds. Top speed was 84 to 85 mph (135 - 136 km/h). The Plymouth was definitely not in the Oldsmobile Rocket 88, or even the Ford V-8 league.

But in spite of its apparent slowness, the Plymouth had lasting qualities. Tom discovered that Bill France, president of the National Association for Stock Car Auto Racing, owned a Suburban. He bought it on the strength of Plymouth's remarkable reliability in regional stock car races; while the hot dogs burned themselves out racing with each other, the little Plymouth just stroked around and often won.

Plymouth was never known as much of an innovator, although it did pioneer "Floating Power" in the form of very soft motor mounts in 1931. It was better known as a sound reliable car that stood up well and provided good value for money, a tradition it retains to this day.

The Suburban, then, fitted Plymouth's image perfectly. It was practical and comfortable, and provided countless years of good transportation for many thousands of families. Although only approximately 20,000 Suburbans were sold during that first year, this was a respectable figure when compared with the sales of wooden wagons.

It wouldn't be very long before the woody wagon would be abandoned and all station wagons would be made of steel. While some General Motors divisions also had all-steel wagons in 1949, it was Plymouth that seemed to offer the best value, and capture the imagination of buyers. It is, therefore, the best remembered of the first all-steel wagons.

PONTIAC GTO

Pontiac was not known as an exciting nameplate during the 1940s and '50s; a good reliable car, yes, but not one likely to get the blood racing. With its Indian-head ornament (the car was named after Chief Pontiac), and garish chrome hood and trunk stripes, they weren't paragons of understated styling taste either. Side-valve six and straight-eight engines provided adequate, if unexciting, performance.

All of that was to change toward the end of the '50s. In 1956 Semon "Bunkie" Knudsen was made general manager of the Pontiac Division of General Motors. Bunkie came to this post with the right blood lines. He was the son of William "Big Bill" Knudsen, who had been GM president from

1964 Pontiac GTO.

– BILL VANCE

1937 to 1940. Bunkie was determined to change Pontiac's image from stodgy to scintillating, and

the way he planned to accomplish it was through improved performance.

A good building block had been provided with the introduction of Pontiac's version of the short-stroke, overhead valve V-8 in 1955. There were also a couple of other important resources available: chief engineer Elliott "Pete" Estes, and assistant chief engineer John De Lorean, both performance car enthusiasts. The first step in their image-changing quest was to provide factory assistance to Pontiacs in National Association for Stock Car Auto Racing (NASCAR) events. NASCAR racing takes place primarily in the southeastern

United States, an evolution of the fast cars and fearless driving required to run moonshine from stills in the piney mountains of places like Wilkes County, North Carolina, down into the towns and cities of the Old South. But while the racing is concentrated in the south, its impact is felt everywhere.

When it was noticed that there was often a high correlation between race wins and car sales, the slogan "Win on Sunday, sell on Monday" was coined. Its meaning was not lost on the Pontiac trio. With the help provided, Pontiac won 30 of the 52 NASCAR Grand National races in 1961 and 22 of the 53 events in 1962. Not coincidentally, it also moved into the third place sales slot right behind Chevrolet and Ford.

In 1963 General Motors placed a corporate ban on factory participation in stock car racing, thus ending Pontiac's fling with NASCAR. Pontiac wanted something to keep its new-found performance image alive, however, so Estes, now general manager, and De Lorean, now chief engineer, started experimenting with their intermediate Tempest model. It had been introduced in 1961, but hadn't enjoyed great sales success.

First they tried one of the division's 326 cubic inch (5.3 litre) V-8 engines in the Tempest and were gratified at the snap it gave the lightweight Pontiac. In the grand Detroit tradition that "if big is good, bigger must be better," they then tried their 389 cubic inch (6.4 litre) V-8 in it, and of course, it was even faster.

Satisfied that they had a winner they decided to offer a GTO (named after a Ferrari model, and standing for Gran Turismo Omologato) option in the redesigned Tempest line for 1964. Not only was it fitted with the big V-8, but it also got heavy duty springs and shocks, and better brakes to handle the higher power. A 4-speed manual transmission was also offered, along with the regular 3-speed manual or 2-speed automatic. All of this activity had been concealed from senior GM management by Estes and De Lorean, and by the time the fourteenth floor found out, it was too late to abort the GTO option. They weren't pleased, however, feeling that it undermined the spirit of the responsible corporate image that GM was trying to project by pulling out of racing. Even Pontiac's general sales manager, Frank Bridges, didn't have much optimism; he refused to include more than 5000 GTOs in the 1964 production schedule.

How wrong he was. Estes and De Lorean, encouraged by Jim Wangers, the account executive with Pontiac's advertising agency, had correctly identified a youth market craving performance. It was the same reservoir that Ford would tap into with its Mustang.

The GTO was an instant sales success and within weeks Pontiac was revamping its production mix to increase the number of GTOs available. GM brass forgot their original unhappiness; they weren't about to put the brakes on a good thing. By the end of the '64 model year 32,450 GTOs had gone out the door, more than six times the estimate of the conservative Mr. Bridges.

The success of the GTO even inspired a song in its honor, "Little GTO" by Ronny and the Daytonas, and choreographed by Wangers. It sold a million records, and the Daytonas then faded almost into obscurity.

Pontiac had started a whole new class of vehicle: the so-called muscle car. And the GTO was indeed muscular. *Car Life* magazine tested a 1965 model with the optional 360 horsepower (standard was 325), triple carburetor "Tri-Power" engine and recorded a zero to 60 mph (96 km/h) time of 5.8 seconds, which is spectacularly fast even by today's standards. Muscle cars were geared for acceleration rather than top speed, and this GTO, with a 4.11:1 axle ratio, was all finished at 114 mph (184 km/h).

Seeing the success of the Pontiac GTO, other manufacturers followed with their own versions. Such cars as the Chevrolet Chevelle SS-396, Oldsmobile 4-4-2, Ford Fairlane GT, Mercury Cyclone GT, Plymouth Road Runner and Dodge Super Bee arrived on the market. Some of these would surpass the GTO in performance as it would lose its edge as the decade progressed.

The muscle car era ended in the early '70s almost as suddenly as it began, killed by brutal

insurance rates and a rising concern over safety. Falling compression ratios and more stringent emissions requirements were also factors that were leading to deteriorating performance. And last but not least, the pony car class of cars spawned by the Ford Mustang, and followed up by the Chevrolet Camaro and Pontiac Firebird, were smaller and nimbler, and could be made just as fast as the muscle cars.

By 1972 the GTO was no longer a separate series, having been folded in with the Pontiac LeMans. It would disappear altogether in 1974. In its 11-year history it had brought scorching performance to the low-priced field, and established the legend of the muscle car. For that it deserves its place in automotive history.

PORSCHE 356

Porsche 356 Speedster.

– BILL VANCE

The lineage of Porsche cars dates back far beyond 1948 when the first prototype Porsche was built. It originated with the People's Car, which German chancellor Adolf Hitler commissioned the Porsche Design Office to develop in the early '30s. This eventually became the Volkswagen Beetle.

Ferdinand Porsche was a brilliant engineer, although he never graduated from engineering school. He was born in 1875 in Bohemia, Austria, the son of a metal worker.

After leaving formal education at age 16, he went to Vienna to apprentice with an electrical company. In the evenings, although not formally registered, he attended engineering lectures at the university in Vienna. Many years later he was delighted to receive an honorary doctorate from the Technical University of Vienna.

An intense interest in the newly emerging automobile prompted young Ferdinand to join the Lohner company, a manufacturer of electric cars, in 1898. By 1900, Porsche had designed his first car for Lohner, the Lohner-Porsche, powered by electric motors integrated into the front wheel hubs. It was an outstanding concept and won a grand prize at the Paris International Exhibition that year.

Porsche's career progressed quickly. He was chief engineer at Austro-Daimler by 1906, then moved on to Daimler-Benz, and Steyr. By 1930 Porsche felt confident enough in his experience

160

and reputation to open his own design shop in Stuttgart. Although he would engineer everything from racing cars to military tanks, his most enduring legacy would be the Volkswagen Beetle, the first prototype of which was completed in 1935.

After World War II, Porsche's health was failing but he yearned to see a car bearing his own name. By now his eldest son, Ferry, was running the company. He had joined the Porsche Design Office when it opened, fresh from completing his engineering apprenticeship with Bosch. And although Ferdinand was a consultant and adviser, it was largely Ferry's effort, and that of close associate Karl Rabe, that went into the first Porsche prototype car completed in the summer of 1948.

That first Porsche was a roadster and it drew heavily on the Volkswagen design and components. It used the VW's four-wheel independent torsion bar suspension, brakes, steering and non-synchromesh transmission.

The horizontally opposed four-cylinder air-cooled engine had the same 1131 cc displacement as the VW, but by raising the compression ratio to 7.0:1, and fitting two carburetors, the engine's output was increased to 40 horsepower from the Beetle's humble 25. The layout of the prototype did vary significantly from the Volkswagen's in one important aspect, however, in that the engine was ahead of the rear axle, not behind it.

Porsche Number 1 was sufficiently successful in road tests that Ferry and his crew went ahead and built a second car in the fall of 1948. This prototype was an aerodynamic coupe, and in order to provide luggage space behind the seats, or even carry a small passenger or two in an emergency, the engine was now mounted behind the rear axle as in the VW. This layout was to become a Porsche trademark that has lasted right up to today.

At about the same time as the second Porsche was completed, the company struck an important deal with Volkswagen. A contract was signed which prohibited Porsche from designing a car for another manufacturer if it would be a direct competitor for the Volkswagen. Also, VW could use Porsche patents if it paid a royalty.

Porsche in return received access to Volkswagen parts, and to the large and rapidly expanding VW sales and service network. This was a breakthrough for the tiny car company because it immediately had at its disposal a soon-too-be worldwide service and distribution system.

Production of the Porsche model 356, as they called the first generation of cars, began in the winter of 1948-49. The first Porsche series was designated 356 because that was its project number in the Porsche shop. But, as Ferry was to admit later, it wasn't their 356th project. In order to give the impression that their new little business was doing well in the beginning, the first consulting job they did was given the number seven, and thus, that first Porsche car was really project number 350.

Initial production was 50 cars, all coupes except six. The car was introduced at the Geneva Motor Show in the spring of 1949, and full-scale production also began at that time in Zuffenhausen on the outskirts of Stuttgart.

Although the first prototypes had been fitted with the same basic 1131 cc engine as the VW, production models were reduced to 1086 cc by way of a 1.5 mm smaller cylinder bore. This brought them within the 1100 cc racing class. In 1951 the 1100 was joined by the 1300 (1286 cc) and the 1500 (1488 cc).

The Porsche 356 was an instant success, a new concept in sports cars, which up to that time had been characterized by uncivilized weather protection, a harsh ride, and generally noisy and heavy operation. Compared with those, the Porsche was like a limousine.

The doors closed with a satisfying clunk and the cabin was snug and comfortable. While not silent, it was at least quieter than the traditional open sports roadster, and the controls were light and convenient. Ride comfort with the four-wheel independent suspension was excellent for a sports car.

A sports car has to prove itself in competition, a point the young company was well aware of; Ferdinand Porsche had been heavily involved in motor racing in the 1930s. A factory-sponsored car was entered in the 1951 Le Mans 24-hour endurance race held annually in France.

Although new and untried, it proved its durability and performance by winning the 1100 cc class, and coming in 20th over-all out of a field of 56, of whom 30 finished. The Porsche was only beaten by cars with much larger engine displacements. It was the beginning of an outstanding competition record for the marque.

The 356 was a sensation when it arrived in North America. *Road & Track* magazine tested a 1500 in November, 1952, and its testers were bowled over. This is, they said, "The car of Tomorrow," and they likened driving it to being at the controls of a small aircraft. It turned in excellent performance for the day, with a zero to 60 mph (96 km/h) acceleration time of 13.8 seconds, and a top speed average of 103.4 mph (165 km/h).

The Porsche 356 went through many variations of the original model and stayed in production until it was succeeded by the 911 model, which was introduced at the Frankfurt Auto Show in 1963. It holds a fond place in many hearts and is a valued collectible today.

ROLLS ROYCE SILVER GHOST

The British Rolls-Royce is claimed, at least by Rolls-Royce Motors of Crewe, Cheshire, to be the best car in the world. Many authorities would dispute that, but most will still admit that it is *one* of the best cars in the world. The model that no doubt did more than any other to establish that reputation was the Silver Ghost, introduced in 1907.

Royce Ltd., a manufacturer of electric motors and generators, started making gasoline engined motor cars in Manchester in 1904. Henry Royce was a meticulous, self-taught engineer, but he felt more at home designing and improving his cars than he did trying to sell them. He needed an extroverted salesman to get out and convince

Rolls Royce Silver Ghost.

— GERRY MALLOY

Charles Stewart Rolls was that kind of man. Born to the aristocracy, the third son of Lord Llangattock, he loved the adventurous life. He flew in balloons and was one of the first to welcome Orville and Wilbur Wright's aeroplane to Europe. (In fact, he was destined to die in a plane accident in 1910 at age 32.) Cars were another of his passions and he became prominent racing them throughout Europe.

He was selling French Panhards in London, and at the urging of a friend, travelled to Manchester in the spring of 1904 to see what Royce had built. Rolls was so impressed with the

buyers of the soundness and engineering excellence he had built into his cars.

car that he immediately suggested that they join forces. A deal was made; Royce would build them and Rolls would sell them.

Up to 1906 Rolls-Royce was trying to find its way as a motor manufacturer. They built several different models with four-and six-cylinder engines, and even a V-8. For 1907 they decided on a one-model policy for the company. This would permit them to concentrate all efforts on developing it, rather than having their resources spread over several models. It was the same policy that Henry Ford would follow with such success with his ubiquitous Model T.

The Silver Ghost was that car, and it debuted at the Olympia Motor Show in November, 1906, designated as a 1907 model. It was a large vehicle, riding on a 135-inch (3442 mm) wheelbase and tipping the scales at 3685 pounds (1675 kg). Power came from a 7-litre inline, side-valve six-cylinder engine that developed 48 horsepower at a leisurely 1200 rpm. Its ultra-high fourth gear, combined with the large wheels, permitted the big six to loaf along at a mere 1000 rpm at 47 mph (76 km/h), a figure unmatched by any modern car.

The "silver" in its name came from the fact that the metal trim parts of the car were silver plated and the body was painted aluminum. The "ghost" implied its quiet operation. Technically, there is only one Rolls-Royce Silver Ghost, that original car, but in practical terms, production

Rolls-Royces were also known as Silver Ghosts.

To demonstrate the new model's engineering quality, it was taken on a 2000-mile (3220 km) reliability run, which included driving from the south coast of England all the way up to Scotland in top gear. This test was conducted under the strict scrutiny of the Royal Automobile Club (R.A.C.).

The car completed the run successfully, but in order to further demonstrate the Ghost's durability, the company immediately sent it out on a 15,000-mile (24,100 km) test, with Charles Rolls as one of the drivers. This, too, was completed without involuntary stops except for tire changes, and it broke the world's record for reliability and long distance.

As final evidence of its superiority, it was then stripped down by R.A.C. engineers to determine how much deterioration it had suffered. Amazingly, there was no wear in the engine, transmission, brakes or steering gear that could be measured with a micrometer.

These exploits established Rolls-Royce's reputation almost overnight and the Silver Ghost model began selling well. The Ghost was built from 1907 to 1925, including some assembled in an American plant in Springfield, Mass., beginning in 1921 (that plant closed in 1931.)

And while it was built for so many years, it is generally conceded that Rolls-Royce's reputation as the maker of the best car in the world was established by the Silver Ghost model between 1907 and the beginning of World War I in 1914.

Incredible as it may seem, the original Silver Ghost test car is still running today. The car was kept around the company during 1907 and part of 1908 where it was used by various officials. In 1908 it was sold to one of Rolls-Royce's travelling inspectors, an A.M. Hanbury, who proceeded to accumulate something in excess of 500,000 miles (804,650 km) on it.

He eventually retired and in 1947 Rolls-Royce received a message from his son-in-law that some spare parts were needed for the Ghost. Hanbury died before the transaction was completed, but Rolls-Royce, now aware of the location of the car, was able to acquire it from the heirs.

Much repair and restoration was required, of course, but Rolls-Royce got it back on the road. It has been serving as a kind of mobile goodwill ambassador for the company ever since, a "working car" as they call it. It has now covered close to 600,000 miles (966,000 km), and it has visited Toronto on its North American tour of selected Rolls-Royce dealerships. Unfortunately, during its visit to Jaguar Rolls-Royce on Bay in Toronto, a small engine bay fire rendered the Ghost *hors de combat* before my turn came for a ride.

I am reliably advised by other journalists who did have an opportunity that the old lady still purrs along very quietly and serenely, that big six

just loafing. Rolls-Royce is fortunate to have its first car, and is to be commended for keeping it on the road, not sitting in a museum somewhere as a static exhibit. I'm sure that Henry Royce and Charles Rolls would have expected no less from the car that launched the legend of "The best car in the world."

EARLY SAABS

As war clouds were gathering over Europe in the mid-1930s, the canny Swedes came to the conclusion that they should have an airplane manufacturing company. Svenska Aeroplan Aktiebolaget, known by the acronym Saab, was therefore established in Trollhattan on the west coast of Sweden in 1937. It was financed by wealthy Swedish businessmen, with the state providing backing for the new enterprise.

Saab had an association with the American aircraft industry from the beginning, and engineers were loaned from several U.S. companies, such as Boeing, to facilitate start-up. Saab would go on to build several American, and even German, planes under licence. By 1939,

1950 Saab 92.

– SAAB

Saab was able to expand by taking over a plant in Linkoping, approximately 280 kilometres (174 miles) south of Stockholm, where it would build planes of its own design.

The aircraft business was successful for Saab, but as the end of World War II approached, the company decided to counter the anticipated decline in its military business by expanding into building automobiles to compete with the other Swedish car company, Volvo. Its aim was also to produce an affordable car for the masses, a kind of "Swedish Volkswagen" that would be simple and sturdy, yet economical to buy and operate.

In 1945, Saab assigned a small staff to one of its aircraft wing design engineers, Gunnar Ljungstrom, and gave the team responsibility for project number 92, the development of the new vehicle. A company technical illustrator by the name of Sixten Sason was called upon to style the body.

Given the background of its designers, it's no surprise that the first prototype Saab's profile came out looking like the cross-section of an airplane wing. The aircraft influence was also evident in the excellent 0.32 coefficient of aerodynamic drag, a figure that is only now being reached by modern cars. With Sweden's relative isolation from the main automobile building countries, and Saab's lack of experience in the business, it's also no surprise that the first Saab came out looking like no other car.

Ljungstrom decided that the car would have front-wheel drive. This decision was apparently not based on any deeply held engineering philosophy, but on the simple reasoning that placing the complete drivetrain in one end of the vehicle seemed like the logical thing to do for both packaging and interior space. It would prove to be a very prescient decision, and a layout that Saab would never deviate from.

Before the war, Ljungstrom had been favorably impressed by the simplicity and soundness of the German DKW car, so he followed the same principle for Saab's powerplant. This decision was also based on the fact that the simple two-stroke design would require less specialized tooling to build.

The first prototype, number 001, was ready by the summer of 1946, a remarkably short time in which to develop an all-new vehicle. It had unit construction, and was powered by a DKW two-cylinder, two-stroke inline water cooled engine mounted laterally in the front of the car. It drove the front wheels through a three-speed transmission. The initial use of the German engine gave Saab time to develop its own design.

Satisfied that the basic engineering was sound, Saab introduced the first production model, designated the 92, to the press in 1947. It would take until 1950 for the Saab 92 to go into production, and only 1246 of them, all green, were built that year.

Based on an announcement (that would subsequently prove too optimistic) by Volvo that it would sell its new PV 444 model for only 4400 kroner (approximately $1100), Saab took some severe cost cutting measures in its original 92. There was, for example, no trunk lid, and only a very small rear window.

That first Saab was, however, what the company had set out to produce: a sturdy, simple and economical little car. It had independent suspension all around using torsion bars, and the tiny 764 cc, 25-horsepower, two-stroke twin could push the two-door, four-passenger sedan to a top speed of some 105 km/h (65 mph), and cruise at 80 to 100 km/h (50 to 62 mph). Lubrication for the engine was achieved by powered by a four-stroke German Ford V-4 engine. But those two-stroke Saabs, in spite of their foibles and peculiarities, are still remembered with fondness for their giant-killer instincts, and their phut-phut-phut exhaust note at idle.

Saab, like the earlier German Volkswagen, and the even earlier American Model T Ford, had started with the premise of building a car that was simple, sturdy and economical. At this they succeeded admirably, which is why they have survived to this day.

mixing oil with the gasoline, which was somewhat of a nuisance, but one that owners seemed willing to accept at that time.

Production gradually increased and by 1954 a total of 10,000 92s had been built. The 92 had given a very early demonstration of its robustness and handling capabilities, and the tractive advantage of front-wheel drive on snow and ice. A few weeks after the first 92 left the factory, Saab's chief test engineer, Rolf Mellde, drove one to victory in the Swedish Winter Rally.

It was the beginning of a long string of rally victories, culminating in its almost invincibility in the early '60s in the hands of Swedish rallyist Eric "on-the-roof" Carlsson who loved to fly over the "yumps." These competition victories, probably more than any other single factor, brought Saab to world attention. Carlsson, happily, is still actively working for Saab.

In 1956 the Saab 93 was introduced, now suspended by coil springs rather than torsion bars. It was fitted with a more powerful three-cylinder engine, again heavily influenced by the German DKW. Its radiator was behind the engine and the fan was driven by a belt and pulley at the front of the engine. This turned a shaft located above the engine, which rotated the rear-mounted fan, leading wags to delight in saying that the Saab had a "single overhead fanshaft."

Saabs started to become more conventional with the 96 model introduced in 1968. It was

STANLEY STEAMER

Steam power should have had a big jump on the gasoline engine when the first spindly, internal combustion engine vehicles lurched into existence in the 1880s. After all, steam had a head start in development of close to 200 years - steam pioneer Thomas Newcomen used one to pump water out of mines in the early 18th century.

The first mechanically motivated road vehicle was a steam tractor built by Nicholas Cugnot in France in 1769. Canada's first automobile, if one could call it that, was a steam-powered buggy built by Henry Seth Taylor of Stanstead, Que. in 1867.

But steam engines had some disadvantages for road-going vehicles. They were, for example,

1906 Stanley Steamer.

– RICHARD SPIEGELMAN

quite heavy for the power they produced, making them more suitable for stationary use, or heavy mobile applications such as locomotives. Also, they required a fairly skilled person to operate them, and they usually took a long time to get up steam and be ready to work. Last, but not least, was the fear of boiler explosion, well-founded or not.

Steam did, of course, have some advantages, the most important of which for a mobile power source was that tremendous torque was available from almost zero crankshaft rpm, thus eliminating the need for a clutch. Thus, a steam engine could accelerate a car quicker, and climb hills far faster than a gasoline-powered vehicle of the era. Gasoline engines, by their nature, had to be spinning over at relatively high rpm before they started to develop much power.

The inherent disadvantages didn't, however, deter some hardy pioneers from pursuing the goal of the steam-powered automobile. Francis E. And Freeland O. Stanley were two of them, and their name, more than any other, would come to be associated with steam cars. They were identical twins who had made a fortune in the dry-plate photography business, starting out in Lewiston, Me. in 1883, and eventually ending up in Boston to be closer to their major markets.

Toward the end of the century they began experimenting with a steam-powered car, but they were disappointed with the weight of the steam engines then available. The engine and boiler they were considering was, at 600 pounds (272 kg), heavier than they had hoped their whole car would be. Undaunted, they set out with the help of an engineering friend, to design their own. The resulting engine weighed a remarkably light 35 pounds (16 kg).

The boiler presented another weight-saving challenge. By constructing a sheet copper shell for the vertical cylindrical pressure vessel, and then wrapping it with piano wire for strength, they developed a boiler that weighed only 125 pounds (57 kg), and could withstand pressures up to 300 pounds per square inch, although they would start out using only 150.

By 1898 the brothers had managed to build three steam cars which they tested extensively around Cambridge, Mass. and their home town of Newton. They sold their first car to a man from Boston that September. When the first Boston automobile show was held in October it included speed and hill-climbing competitions which the Stanley won easily, including successfully scaling a 30 percent grade.

This was the start the Stanleys needed, and the orders started to pour in. An empty factory next to their photography plant was acquired, and within a year of their first sale it was estimated that as many as 200 cars had been made.

As did other cars of the day, the Stanley drew extensively on carriage and bicycle technology. The engine was under the seat with the vertical boiler behind it. A chain carried the power to the rear axle, and tiller steering was used.

The Stanleys' success attracted the interest of one John B. Walker, publisher of *Cosmopolitan* magazine, who wanted to buy the business. To dissuade this persistent suitor, the Stanleys finally named a price they thought ridiculously high: a quarter million dollars in cash. Walker promptly paid it and the Stanleys found themselves out of the car business. The new owner changed the name to the Locomobile Company of America.

By 1901 they were manufacturing steam cars again, but were promptly sued by George

Whitney, another steam-car maker, for infringement of his chain tensioner patent. Undaunted, the Stanleys quickly changed their design and placed the engine horizontally in the rear of the car, driving the axle with a gear drive, a better system.

One of the first people to exploit the steamer's performance potential was Louis Ross, of Newtonville, Mass. He fitted his streamlined "Wogglebug" with two boilers and two Stanley engines and achieved a stunning 94.7 mph (152 km/h) on the sands of Ormond Beach, Fla. in 1905.

Encouraged by this feat, the Stanleys constructed a special car that company driver Fred Marriott drove to a new land speed record of 127.6 mph (205 km/h) in January, 1906. Although Marriott crashed at an estimated 242 km/h (150 mph) in 1907, fortunately not fatally, while trying to better his own record, his 1906 speed would stand as the record for several years.

The company expanded its line into a wide variety of models, becoming best known for the "coffin nose" hood shape that housed the cylindrical boiler. The gasoline engine was making steady strides, however, improving in durability and reliability with every new model.

The introduction of the electric starter on the Cadillac gasoline engine in 1912 marked the beginning of the end for the steam car. The internal combustion engine was now released from its most encumbering trait: the need to be started with a difficult and dangerous hand crank.

Stanley continued to build cars on through the teens but the gasoline engine was rapidly improving and the Stanley didn't always have the latest in steam technology. Bankruptcy was declared in 1923. The company was reorganized as the Steam Vehicle Corp. of America in 1924, but was out of the car business for good by about 1925.

STUDEBAKER HAWKS

Studebaker Hawk 1959-61.

– BERT COATES

The Studebaker name holds a lot of good memories for many people. Although they ceased building cars in 1966 (they were last produced in Hamilton, Ont.), the enterprise that was formed in 1852 by Henry and Clement Studebaker in South Bend, Ind., to build farm wagons has, over the years, turned out some exciting models.

Among these were the Studebaker Hawks produced from 1956 to 1964. The Hawk series owed its origin to the lovely Starlight and Starliner coupes introduced as 1953 models. When *Road & Track* magazine tested the Studebaker Commander coupe in September, 1953, they called it "The American car with the European look." In 1955 the President name was revived by Stude-

baker after 13 years of dormancy, and the Starlight coupe evolved into the President Speedster.

The Speedster lasted only one year, and in 1956 was used as the basis for the Hawk series of coupes. Hawks came in four models: the Flight Hawk, Power Hawk, and Sky Hawk, based on Studebaker Champion, Commander and President trim levels respectively. At the very top of the hierarchy was the Golden Hawk. All Hawks had the longer 120.5 inch (3048 mm) President Classic wheelbase rather than the 116.6 inch (2959 mm) one of the other models. The Golden Hawk was loaded with equipment, and in addition, was loaded with power.

The Studebaker Corp. and the Packard Motor

172

Car Co. had merged in 1954 to become the Studebaker-Packard Corp. Along with its cars and a grand old name, Packard brought to the wedding its big 352 cubic inch (5.8 litre) overhead valve V-8. It developed 275 horsepower and was the powerplant used for the Golden Hawk. The extra 100 pounds (45 kg) added to the front end of the coupe made it pretty nose-heavy, which placed severe compromises on handling and braking. In spite of its forward weight bias, it would accelerate fiercely in a straight line; Studebaker-Packard claimed in its advertising that it would go from zero to 60 mph (96 km/h) in 8.7 seconds, which was quite quick for the era.

Many felt, however, that the Power Hawk with the Studebaker 259 cubic inch (4.2 litre) V-8, or the Sky Hawk with the 289 (4.7 litre) V-8, were better all-round choices, although they lacked the brute force power of the Packard-engined Hawk.

The lesser coupes had another advantage too; they didn't get those bolt-on fibreglass fins that the Golden Hawk did, at least not for 1956, and thus had much cleaner rear-end styling. It wouldn't last for long, however, as the fin fad of the '50s soon swept all before it.

For 1957 the Hawk line was reduced to two nameplates, the Golden Hawk and the Silver Hawk, the Sky, Power and Flight Hawks having disappeared. The choice was still wide, however, because the Silver Hawk could be had with the uninspired 170 cubic inch (2.8 litre) side-valve six, which had powered the Flight Hawk in 1956, or the two Studebaker V-8s.

The biggest engine change came in the Golden Hawk, which lost the heavy Packard V-8 in favor of Studebaker's own 289 cub c inch (4.7 litre) V-8. But power couldn't be allowed to slip in a prestige car in those horsepower race days, so to keep the 275 horsepower rating Studebaker-Packard mounted a belt-driven, centrifugal supercharger on the engine.

Things continued largely unchanged for 1958 except that Packard got its oar in the water in the form of the Packard Hawk. It was virtually identical to the Golden Hawk mechanically, but had rather bizarre styling with a low sloping nose, fake spare tire molded into the trunk lid, and padded arm rests on the *outside* of the doors for those drivers who liked to drape their arm out the window. The Packard Hawk lasted just one model year with a mere 588 being produced. If it has any collectible value today, it's probably more for its rarity than for its aesthetics.

By 1959 the series was down to the Silver Hawk only, available with the 259 (4.2 litre) V-8 or the six. For 1960 and 1961 the car continued largely unchanged, although the name, starting in 1960, was simply the Hawk. The six-cylinder engine was converted to overhead valves in 1961 and horsepower rose from 9) to 112 out of the same 170 cubic inches (2.8 litres). It was an academic point, however, because no new six-cylinder Hawks were sold in North America after the 1959 model year, although some were exported.

Hawk sales had been on a slide. The best year had been 1957 when 19,674 were produced, but by 1959 this was down to only 7888, and for 1960, an even worse 4507. When sales fell to 3929 in 1961 something clearly had to be done. Either the line had to be rejuvenated or the model dropped altogether.

Studebaker chose to try to wring a few more years out of it and engaged the services of a well known Milwaukee designer by the name of Brooks Stevens. Stevens lived up to his reputation and produced a very nice restyling job, which required little in the way of new tooling, something the cash-strapped company couldn't afford.

By giving it a squared up, more formal roof line, knocking off those 1957-61 rear fins, and adding a few styling tricks here and there, Stevens produced an attractive and fresh looking design. They called it the Gran Turismo Hawk and it did the trick on the sales floor. Production jumped to 9335 for 1962.

By 1963 it was clear that Studebaker was in trouble financially, and the Hawk suffered along with the rest of the line. The GT Hawk remained basically the same until it was discontinued with the failure of Studebaker-Packard's American car-building operation in November 1963, and the

production of remaining Studebaker models was moved to Canada, where it would continue until March 1966.

The Hawk is fondly remembered by many, particularly the surprisingly large number of Studebaker fans still around. Richard Griggs of Scarborough, treasurer of the Ontario chapter of the Studebaker Drivers Club, advises me that there are over 150 members in the Ontario chapter, and approximately 11,000 worldwide.

TAYLOR STEAM BUGGY
1867

What is credited as being Canada's first engine-powered road vehicle was built by Henry Seth Taylor, fittingly, in 1867, the year Canada became a nation. Although it appeared 19 years before Karl Benz patented his gasoline-powered car in 1886, it was propelled by a steam engine, and is thus not considered a genuine pioneer of the modern gasoline automobile.

Henry Taylor was born on April 9, 1831 on a farm near Stanstead Plain, as Stanstead was then known, in the Eastern Townships of Quebec. Stanstead is on the Vermont border some 150 kilometres (93 miles) southeast of Montreal. After serving his apprenticeship in Boston, Taylor returned and set up as a watchmaker in Stanstead.

Taylor Steam Buggy 1867.

– CARS OF CANADA

It was a good place to be interested in mechanically powered vehicles. Although the majority of Canadian automaking is now based in Ontario, the Eastern Townships area, possibly because of its proximity to New England, could be called a kind of birthplace of the Canadian automobile. In addition to Taylor, it also yielded George Foote Foss, builder of Canada's first gasoline-powered car in 1897, and Joseph Armand Bombardier of snowmobile fame.

As befits a watchmaker, Taylor was a meticulous craftsman and an inveterate tinkerer. Perhaps through his exposure to American steam buggies, or from observing steam locomotives, he became interested in building a steam powered vehicle. The basis for his "car," which he started building in 1865 with the assistance of blacksmith Joseph Mosher, was a high-wheeled carriage to which they added some bracing to support an engine.

To power it he chose a horizontal, two-cylinder steam engine with a bore and stroke of 3.5 by 10.0 inches (89 by 254 mm). It was mounted amidships under the floor, with the long connecting rods extending back and attaching directly to the rear axle, which therefore also acted as the engine's crankshaft.

Steam was generated in a coal-fired vertical boiler mounted at the rear of the vehicle behind the seat. It was connected by rubber hoses to a six-gallon (27 litre) water tank located between the front wheels. The large vertical stack set at a jaunty angle gave it a decidedly locomotive-like appearance.

Forward and reverse movements were controlled by a lever, and the car was steered by a long cogged rack that extended back from the wheels, and was acted on by a gear actuated by a vertical shaft topped by a crank. It was a kind of early version of rack-and-pinion steering. A ratchet mechanism on the rear axle provided differential action. It was quite a complete little vehicle, except that it had no brakes; Henry apparently thought that he wouldn't be travelling fast enough to require them.

The Taylor's public debut, unfortunately, turned out to be somewhat of a debacle. He drove it onto the exhibition field at the 1867 Stanstead Fall Fair, only to have a steam hose rupture and envelope Henry and his car in steam. He had to unceremoniously push his little 500 pound (277 kg) buggy off the field to the hoots and catcalls of the audience. According to the report of the incident in the *Stanstead News*, "This...breaking down of the car, were contretemps detracting somewhat from the interest of the occasion."

Henry was disappointed, but not deterred. He continued to work on and drive his little steam buggy. It reportedly operated very successfully and he exhibited it at several Eastern Townships and New England fairs. He ventured as far as St. Johnsbury, Vermont, a distance of 50 miles (80 km), to exhibit it at their fair where, according to his grandson, "it scared all the horses and the ladies." There was talk of suing Taylor, but this was probably a threat made more in jest than in earnest.

Alas, Henry was a man ahead of his time and there seemed to be little enthusiasm for his invention among fellow citizens. Despite apathy and occasional ridicule, he continued to drive his car well into the 1870s. It has been widely reported that one day he misjudged his speed on a hill. The car is said to have got out of control and Henry had to jump clear and let it crash, which broke at least two wheels. Whether this story is true or not, Taylor eventually stored it in a loft, and seemed to have lost interest.

Taylor later removed the steam engine and installed it in a launch called the *Gracie*. It was said to be the first steam powered boat to ply the waters of Lake Memphremagog.

Time passed, and so did Mr. Taylor, on January 7, 1887. During his lifetime he had never bothered to patent his steam buggy. The remains of it had lain dormant for over 70 years when the property came into the hands of Taylor's grandson, H.A. Taylor in 1948. The pieces in the loft had continued to slumber, apparently disturbed only by a scrap metal dealer during World War II who, luckily, decided that they were more trouble to remove than they were worth. He took a plough instead.

The property, including the buggy remains, was sold to a Mrs. Gertrude Snowden of Stanstead in 1960. Fortunately she recognized that she had something of value, and offered the buggy to several museums who showed no interest. It was eventually sold to an American named Mr. Richard M. Stewart. He was the president of Anaconda American Brass in Connecticut, and had an interest because of the brass content in the engine. He set out to have it restored with nothing more than the original metal parts and some old photos to go by. It was brought back to original condition, with the exception of a different boiler and the addition of brakes.

Amazingly, after almost 100 years of dormancy, the brass cylinders and many of the engine parts were still usable. Restoration consisted of fitting new wheels, a boiler and the leather and wood body parts. Mr. Stewart drove it on several occasions, usually using compressed air for short trips, and steaming up for longer ones.

Recognizing the significance of the vehicle in Canadian history, Mr. Stewart allowed it to be placed on display in the Ontario Science Centre in Toronto for several years. Fortunately the Taylor steam buggy came back into Canadian hands when it was purchased by the National Museum of Science and Technology in Ottawa in 1983. This is to be its permanent home.

It is ironic that it fell to an American to re-store this valuable Canadian artifact, which is recognized as Canada's first car. Perhaps, though, it is fitting in a way because Henry Seth Taylor lived in Vermont, some 400 yards across the border in Derby Line. It was during this period that he built his little steam buggy in Stanstead. This monument to Mr. Taylor's pioneering spirit and ingenuity is on display in the National Museum of Science and Technology in Ottawa.

TRIUMPH TR2

1954 Triumph TR2.

– BILL VANCE

The Triumph Cycle Co. Ltd., of Coventry, England, later to become the Triumph Motor Co. Ltd., a famous motorcycle builder, decided to go into the automobile manufacturing business in 1923. The nameplate was relatively unknown in North America, however, until the 1950s. The car that was to really set its reputation in motion over here was a rather snub-nosed roadster known as the TR2. It was developed on a low budget, and equipped with an engine that was so robust it was also used to power the Ferguson farm tractor.

The TR2 owed its origin to Sir John Black, managing director of the Standard Motor Co. Ltd. Using components scavenged from the corporate parts bin, he had a prototype sport roadster built. It was called the Triumph TR1 and was shown to the world at the 1952 London Motor Show. The TR2 evolved directly from this car.

The story had all started much earlier. Although Standard had been supplying chassis and engines to William Lyons, father of the Jaguar, before World War II, Black had still viewed Lyons as a competitor. Black's ambition was to go head-to-head with Lyons in the sports car field. To pursue this he bought the bombed out Triumph factory in 1944, and announced that he would produce a new sports car after the war. Triumph had established a good sporty car reputation before the war with such models as the Southern Cross, Gloria and Dolomite, but after the war, Black wanted more.

His first post-war effort in the open-car market had been the classically styled Triumph 1800 Roadster. This was a tubular-framed, aluminum and wood-bodied model powered by the same 1.8 litre engine that Black had been selling to Lyons in the '30s. It was produced for two years, 1946-1947, and then evolved into the 2000 Roadster through the fitting of a 2.1 litre overhead-valve four. This was the same newly developed wet-sleeve engine that was used in the Ferguson tractor, and also in the new Standard Vanguard sedan and the Morgan sports car.

The 2000 Roadster was built during 1948 and '49, but it and the 1800 were really not sports cars; they were rather more like a gentleman's touring. Their performance was modest, but they did have one unique feature that set them apart: they were fitted with rumble seats, "dickey seats," the British called them, the last to be offered in a production car.

When Lyons introduced his bombshell Jaguar XK120 model late in 1948 it was immediately apparent to Black that he may as well abandon any notions of competing directly with his old foe. But Lyons did, in a way, open up an opportunity for Black. His new Jaguar created a gaping chasm in the sports car market between the angular, outdated MG T models, and the high performance XK120.

After an abortive attempt with a fully envelope-bodied roadster designated TR-X and nicknamed the Bullet, Black set to work in earnest on the car that would become the TR1, and ultimately the TR2.

Triumph chief engineer Ted Grinham took the sturdy Vanguard/Ferguson engine and dropped it into the chassis of the prewar Flying Standard. The coil spring front suspension came from the little knife-edge styled Triumph Mayflower. The Vanguard provided the transmission, which was changed from a 3-speed to a 4-speed, and modified to take the Laycock de Normanville electric overdrive unit.

A meagre 16,000 pounds (about $65,000 at that time) was provided for the body tooling, which meant that designer Walter Belgrove had little room for very imaginative styling. The trick was to avoid expensive compound curves, and thus, such expedients were used as splitting the front fenders along the centre line and filling the seams with beading, although a bright trim strip was later added.

The only compound body pressings were the headlamps, which were almost progenitors of those on the later Bug-Eye Austin-Healey Sprites. Another cost-saving move was the use of external hinges everywhere but on the doors. And not much was spent on the tiny egg-crate grille. It was quite a small car, riding on an 88 inch (2235 mm) wheelbase, and weighing just over 2000 pounds

(907 kg) when it reached the market.

All in all, it looked far better than it had any right to, given the minuscule body budget. The first TR1 shown had a bobbed off rear end with the spare tire mounted externally, Continental style. Lengthening the tail and stowing the spare under the trunk floor much improved the appearance of the TR2, which was introduced at the Geneva Motor Show in March, 1953.

Performance, of course, is what a sports car is all about, and here the TR2 didn't disappoint. Engineer Grinham and race driver Ken Richardson went to work on the sturdy but underpowered (68 horsepower) Vanguard engine. They reduced the displacement slightly from 2.0 litre to 1991 to bring it within the 2.0-litre racing class. They then beefed up the necessary parts such as the cylinder head mounting studs, and gradually got it up to 90 horsepower through such modifications as twin carburetors, a higher lift cam and higher compression.

To demonstrate its performance, Ken Richardson fitted a TR2 with a bellypan, metal tonneau cover, small racing windshield, and rear fender skirts (an early option), and headed for the famous Jabbeke Highway in Belgium. This was Europe's equivalent to the Utah salt flats, and a place where, *Mechanix Illustrated's* Tom McCahill used to joke, even a kid on roller skates could go 50 mph (80 km/h).

Richardson's first run was a very disappointing 104.86 mph (169 km/h). There were a lot of long faces around the car until it was discovered that a spark plug wire had become disconnected; the attempt had been made on three cylinders! Running on all four, Richardson achieved an excellent 124.095 mph (200 km/h) over the flying mile, and 124.889 mph (201 km/h) over the flying kilometre.

The stock TR2 also turned in outstanding performance when it reached North America and was tested by *Road & Track* magazine in its April '54 issue. They recorded a zero to 60 mph (96 km/h) time of 12.2 seconds ("the TR2 will out-drag any American car") and a top speed of 103 mph (166 km/h), virtually identical to the 2.7-litre-engined, and more expensive, Austin-Healey 100.

The Triumph quickly established an enthusiastic following based on its sturdiness, relatively low price, and excellent performance. It won many race and rally honors on both sides of the Atlantic and soon established itself as the dominant force in the 2.0-litre sports car class.

TR2s were made from 1953 to 1955 during which time 8636 were built. They are now probably the most sought-after of all Triumph models and a man lucky enough to have an excellent one is Ray Spencer of Scarborough, Ontario. He is an enthusiastic member of the Toronto Triumph Club, and enjoys pampering his '54 model and driving it to club meets both locally and in the U.S.A.

THE
LakeErieBeacon

The Lake Erie Community Newspaper

Linda Hibbert
MARKETING ADVISOR

204 A Carlow Road Port Stanley, ON N5L 1C5

519.782.4563   linda@lebeacon.ca

TUCKER

1948 Tucker.

— RICHARD SPIEGELMAN

One of the most bizarre and yet fascinating chapters of automotive history was written by Preston Tucker in the years just after World War II. Tucker's plan was to manufacture a revolutionary car, a car that would be so advanced it would make everything else on the road obsolete. His story has prompted books, countless articles, and even a movie.

Among those who remember Tucker and his car, there is a wide range of opinion. There are the true believers who say he was a genuine entrepreneur in the mold of Billy Durant (founder of General Motors), while others think he was a flimflamming fraud only intent on fleecing the public.

Tucker was born in 1901 and raised in the Detroit suburb of Lincoln Park. Motor City had a powerful influence on him. His size — six foot two, 200 pounds - and easy manner made him a natural salesman. He spent some of his career selling cars, then as a police officer. He was a regional representative for the Pierce-Arrow company, a manufacturer of luxury cars.

Auto racing fascinated Tucker, and in 1929 he crossed paths with Harry Miller, a famous race car builder whose front-drive racers dominated the Indy 500 in the late twenties and early thirties. Miller would give Tucker some of the ideas that he would later use in his car.

The two formed a partnership to try to take

over Marmon, an Indianapolis luxury car manufacturer that was failing under the economic weight of the Depression. That didn't materialize, but it did convince Tucker that he wanted to manufacture his own car someday.

Tucker continued to wheel and deal. With war looming in Europe, he developed a fast combat car fitted with a rotary gun turret which he demonstrated to the army. They said they didn't need the 117 mph (188 km/h) speed, but that they could use the turret.

This was Tucker's signal. By 1940 he had established a successful machine shop business in Ypsilanti, near Detroit, to build turrets. It grew into the Tucker Aviation Corp. and prospered during World War II by manufacturing them. The end of the war brought the end of that business, which freed Tucker to pursue his dream of building his own car.

In December 1945 Tucker announced his plan to bring out his futuristic new car. The specifications were fantastic; it really did sound like "The Car of Tomorrow." The Tucker Torpedo, later renamed the 48, was to be a large, low, 6-passenger sedan with a big, 6-cylinder aluminum engine in the rear.

At a time when established motor manufacturers were struggling to resume post-war production of pre-war designs, Tucker was promising a car-starved nation an aerodynamically efficient vehicle capable of cruising at 100 mph (160 km/h). It would have many advanced safety features such as a "pop-out" windshield, and disc brakes. Suspension would be independent all around using a new "Torsilastic" system that combined rubber and torsion bars. And it would be sold at a very affordable price.

The Tucker's engine was to drive the rear wheels through a torque converter on each end of the crankshaft - an idea that probably led to the later rumors that the car wouldn't back up. The extremely slow-turning engine promised excellent fuel economy, and indeed, would have been capable of 100 mph cruising without any engine worries.

By the end of 1946 Tucker knew that to be successful in obtaining financial backing he needed more than drawings and pictures of his new car. He commissioned Alex Tremulus, a noted aircraft designer, to design and build a prototype within the incredibly short time of 100 days. It was a Herculean task, but Tremulus and crew accomplished it.

The prototype was built on an Oldsmobile chassis by a skilled group of Indianapolis 500 racing mechanics. During this hectic period the car was affectionately dubbed the "Tin Goose," a term that would be used derogatorily against the car and Tucker in later court cases.

Many of the original ideas, such as the transverse engine and the torque converters, had to be abandoned as unworkable. And the car was much more conservatively styled than the original drawings, although it was still quite low and very advanced.

The safety windshield and padded dash were retained, but the front fenders that turned with the wheels were gone, as were the disc brakes. A third centre-mounted "cyclops eye" headlamp that steered with the wheels survived. The engine, now a much smaller 334 cubic inch (5.5 litre) aluminum helicopter powerplant, converted from air to water cooling, drove the car through a Cord preselector transmission.

Tucker was able to finance his operation by the unorthodox method of pre-selling dealer franchises, followed by the successful mounting of a $20 million stock offering. He acquired a huge war surplus bomber engine plant in Chicago on very favorable terms because the War Assets Administration was anxious to unload it. Preston Tucker was in the business of building cars, or so he thought.

Not long after his acquisition, the Securities and Exchange Commission - the U.S. federal stock trading watchdog - began to look askance at his dealer franchise sales. Tucker Corp. stock collapsed and he was able to stay afloat only by pre-selling such accessories as radios and seat covers for the cars.

Through all of the charges and counter-charges that were flying around, the plant managed to turn out 51 cars in 1948, before the

end finally came in 1949. Tucker was later cleared of all charges but it was too late; the damage had been done. There would be no more Tucker cars.

The cars themselves were reportedly surprisingly good, considering the circumstances under which they were built. Tom McCahill of *Mechanix Illustrated* magazine, America's original car tester, reported in the August, 1948, issue that the one he tried would accelerate from zero to 60 mph (96 km/h) in 10 seconds, and top 105 mph "the quickest 105 mph I have ever reached."

He also reported that the Tucker was "roomy and extraordinarily comfortable," and that "it steers and handles better than any American car I have driven. As to roadability" he went on, "it's in a class by itself." Even allowing for a touch of "Uncle Tom's" famed hyperbole, the cars sounded very good.

Tucker's brave attempt to crack the Detroit establishment had failed. There is a Tucker owner's club dedicated to keeping the faith, and keeping the remaining Tuckers on the road.

Preston Tucker always claimed that he was the victim of dark conspiratorial Detroit interests who were genuinely afraid his advanced new car would undermine the establishment. He died of cancer in Ypsilanti on Dec. 26, 1956 carrying that belief to his grave. A fully restored Tucker car can be seen in the auto museum of the Imperial Palace in Las Vegas, Nev.

VOLKSWAGEN BEETLE

1967 Volkswagen Beetle.

– BILL VANCE

In a world now populated by sleek, front-engine, front-wheel drive small cars, it's hard to believe that the most popular little car on the road 30 years ago was a rear-engine, rear-wheel drive, blunt-nosed machine that had been designed away back in the 1930s. I am speaking, of course, of the Volkswagen Beetle.

At first blush it was a most unlikely candidate to become the most popular car in the world, to ultimately far surpassing the production of even the legendary Model T Ford.

The VW story began in 1933 when Adolf Hitler became chancellor of Germany. Among his Depression projects was a network of super highways, the autobahns, which would criss-cross the country. To complement these new roads, he asked the German auto manufacturers to build a sturdy, economical small car that the average German burgher could afford. Hitler was an admirer of Henry Ford and what he had done to motorize North America. He wanted Germans to enjoy the same freedom. The vehicle was to accommodate a family of four or five, be low in initial cost, and be able to cruise all day at 100 km/h (62 mph) on Germany's new highway system.

When established carmakers like Mercedes-Benz and Auto Union didn't respond, Hitler vowed he would go it alone with a state-backed program to develop a car for the masses.

184

Ferdinand Porsche, a brilliant automotive engineer who ran his own consulting engineering company called the Porsche Design Office, was commissioned to design the small car. Not one to reinvent the wheel if he didn't need to, Porsche took a still-born design he had developed for the NSU company and used it as the basis for the Hitler car.

The first prototype, built in Porsche's private garage in Stuttgart, emerged late in 1935. It had a horizontally opposed (flat), air-cooled, four-cylinder engine mounted behind the rear axle. Power reached the rear wheels through a four-speed manual overdrive transmission. All four wheels were independently suspended using torsion bars. The body was a beetle-shaped, two-door sedan that was quite aerodynamically efficient for its time.

Two more prototypes were built, and 150,000 km (93,000 miles) of open-road testing with the three cars found them to be acceptable, if not entirely problem-free. They met the 100 km/h cruising goal without distress and achieved an adequate 40 miles per gallon. Hitler was satisfied, and ordered the carmakers to produced 60 of his new babies, of which 30 were used for further testing and 30 for propaganda purposes.

Hitler wanted to call the car the KdF-wagen (from Kraft durch Freude, or Strength through Joy), but the public quickly dubbed it simply the People's Car, or Volkswagen, and the name stuck.

185

Following two million more kilometres of testing, the Volkswagen was ready for production in 1937. Hitler again turned to the industry, this time to mass produce his car, and again it resisted. Exasperated, he established a huge factory in Lower Saxony near Wolfsburg castle; the town that grew up around it would become Wolfsburg. He even initiated a pre-payment plan whereby Germans in effect paid for their cars in advance through a system of savings stamps. World War II brought an end to that program, but it would return to haunt the company after the war. Following an 11-year lawsuit brought by Volkswagen stamp-savers the case would finally be settled in 1961.

By the time the plant was completed in 1939, Hitler was engaged in far more sinister activities, and the factory soon shifted to producing Jeep-like military vehicles. These were based on Volkswagen components and were called Kubelwagens ("bucket cars") in the land version, and Schwimmwagens in the amphibious version. The end of World War II would find the plant largely in ruins from Allied bombing.

The plant was under the control of the British who were using it as a truck repair depot. They were anxious to see something done with it, and were ready to welcome workers who gradually drifted back and began finding the car building machinery and cleaning up the plant. They were soon able to begin building a trickle of cars; 1785 were produced in 1945, which were used by the occupying forces and the German Post Office. This increased to 10,020 in 1946, and then slipped back to 8987 in '47.

The Allies didn't know what to do with the huge plant. They offered it to the Ford Motor Co., and to Hillman of England, both of whom looked at the ugly, rough riding little car and declined. Ernest Breech, a senior Ford official was particularly blunt: he said it was "not worth a damn." The British motor industry suggested that the plant be razed.

The turning point came in 1948 when an experienced automotive engineer by the name of Heinz Nordhoff took over the management of the plant. If there was a saviour for Volkswagen, it was Nordhoff. He was tough and dedicated. He moved his cot into the office so he could sleep there for a few months to be on top of the business. When workers demanded higher wages he told them bluntly that their demands would sink the entire enterprise. He reported company fortunes to staff quarterly, and his honesty and drive raised morale and won them over.

Production boomed. By May, 1949, a total of 50,000 Beetles had been built. That figure reached 100,000 by March, 1950, 500,000 by July, 1953 and one million by August, 1955.

Nordhoff knew that Volkswagen had to export to prosper. The first Beetles to be officially imported to North America came in 1949 when a Dutch entrepreneur named Ben Pon brought two into the United States. The first VWs officially imported to Canada were 1953 models brought in by Volkswagen Canada in 1952.

Backed by a good dealer network, the sturdy VW Beetle gradually became the best-selling imported car in North America. For several years it sold well without any advertising, but when it did become necessary, Doyle Dane Burnbach of New York came up with some of the most clever and effective ads since Ned Jordan hawked his Jordan Playboys with "Somewhere West of Laramie." Who can forget, for example, the one entitled "Did you ever wonder how the snow-plough driver gets to work?"

The Beetle's time would eventually pass, of course. It gradually became technically obsolete. In the '70s the shift came to front-wheel drive, and buyers chose more modern styling and performance.

The Volkswagen Beetle was recently chosen as the Car of the Century by an international group of automotive journalists. It was a fitting tribute, and a testimony to the soundness of the original design that Ferdinand Porsche laid down back in the 1930s. The VW Beetle was kept in production in various parts of the world as long as there was a demand, and is still being produced in Mexico. Over 22 million have been built.

VOLKSWAGEN VAN

A great deal of the credit for the popularity of the minivan must go to the Chrysler Corp. Its T-115 "Magic Wagons," as they love to call them, came on the scene for 1984 as the Dodge Caravan and Plymouth Voyager. They were an immediate success and became immensely popular, so popular that Chrysler still dominates the field.

This has led many to believe that Chrysler invented a whole new class of vehicle. But while they may have made it a household item, it is Volkswagen that really deserves the credit for originating our modern version of the minivan. We should note that a clever automotive engineer named William Stout conceived a

Volkswagen Van (1st generation.)

–VOLKSWAGEN CANADA

somewhat similar rear-engined vehicle which he called the Scarab back in the 1930s, but it never caught on. Perhaps it was just too far ahead of its time, or perhaps the world wasn't ready to accept its Art Deco styling.

The genesis of the modern minivan goes back to 1950. Volkswagen was still recovering from the ravages inflicted on its huge Wolfsburg plant during World War II. With Beetle production well under way - 1950 would see the 100,000th produced - VW decided to move into the commercial field.

The concept was a basic one. Starting with a ladder-type frame, VW's engineers constructed the largest possible vehicle using the same 94.5-

inch (2400 mm) wheelbase as the Beetle. The van's 165-inch (4191 mm) length was only five inches (127 mm) longer than that of the car.

Not surprisingly, the result looked very much like a box. It had a flat front, an almost horizontal steering wheel and a front seat mounted directly above the wheels. This was really cab forward, long before Chrysler used the term to describe its popular LH sedans (Chrysler Concorde, et al.).

Access to the cargo area was through two swinging doors on the right side, plus a hatch at the rear. VW had struck on a very clever concept. The van's compact dimensions, huge volume (170 cubic feet, or nearly five cubic metres), high manoeuvrability and curb-side door openings made it ideally suited for a wide variety of light delivery duties. It had a carrying capacity of three-quarters of a ton, and was really in a class by itself.

The VW Transporter, or Type 2 (its official designation) was powered by the same 30-horsepower, 1.2 litre, air-cooled, four cylinder, horizontally opposed (flat) engine as the Beetle. It was, as in the sedan, located behind the rear axle and drove the rear wheels through a four-speed manual transmission. Suspension was independent all around via torsion bars.

To increase ground clearance and provide pulling power to cope with the van's 2430 pounds (1105 kilograms), a weight far greater than the sedan's, reduction gears were fitted at each driving wheel hub. These served the purpose, although the combination of gear whine and the noisy engine created a terrible din in the uninsulated metal box.

These gears also made the engine run faster than the car's for a given road speed. And since VW's engineers weren't comfortable turning the little flat four much over 3500 rpm, the instrument panel carried this warning: "The allowable top speed of this vehicle is 50 mph" (80 km/h), an admonition usually disregarded.

Volkswagen soon expanded the line from the original utilitarian van and window van to a luxurious little nine-passenger bus called the Kombi, or Microbus. There were other versions, too, including a pickup truck, a camper and even an ambulance. The addition of seats, carpets and sound insulation reduced the gear and engine sound to a distant, almost inaudible thrum.

As might be expected with such a small engine propelling a vehicle of this weight, performance could best be described as modest. *Road & Track* magazine tested a VW Microbus (now up to 36 hp) in its December, 1956, issue and recorded a top-speed average of 59 mph (95 km/h), with a best run of 60 (96).

Acceleration to 60 (96) was largely academic, but was reported as 75 seconds. Zero to 50 (80) took 30.6 seconds. Fuel economy was quite respectable, however, at 26 to 29 mpg U.S. (31 to 35 Imperial).

Volkswagen had the microbus field almost to

itself for over a decade. Then in 1961, Chevrolet and Ford brought out rival versions, with Dodge following in 1964.

In its Corvair 95 Greenbrier minivan, Chevrolet chose, as it had with the Corvair car, to follow the VW configuration by using a flat, air-cooled engine located in the rear. As with the VW, the two American vehicles used car components. the Greenbrier's coming from the Corvair, and the Econoline's from the compact Falcon. The Econoline van was, therefore a conventional front engine, rear drive layout. This reduced convenience somewhat by placing the engine between the two front seats. Both would also spin off pickup variations.

The arrival of the American challengers to the VW's lead naturally invited comparison. *Car Life* magazine conducted a three-way test of the VW, Greenbrier and Econoline in its Sept. 1961 issue. Each manufacturer used different nomenclature for its vehicle. VW called its van a Station Wagon, Chevrolet called the Greenbrier a Sports Wagon, and Ford's was a Station Bus.

The magazine found that while they were all basically a box on wheels, each had its own character. The VW was the most economical, the Greenbrier the most comfortable, and the Ford Econoline the fastest. Speed was perhaps an oxymoron to describe the three. The VW (now listed as 40 hp) could barely struggle up to 60 mph (96 km/h), the Chevrolet to 70 (113), and

the Ford to 75 (121).

Acceleration was equally leisurely. The VW was not rated from zero to 60 mph (96 km/h) because it simply took so long with a light breeze or slight incline it would not reach it at all. The Greenbrier did it in 32.2 seconds, while the Ford took 25.8. In the zero to 50 test, the VW's small engine again showed up with time of 26.8 against the Chev's 19.6 and the Ford's 16.2.

The VW van was a brilliant concept, a pioneering vehicle that pointed the way for all the rest. Like the pioneering BMC Mini, it provided the maximum carrying capacity in the most compact possible dimensions. It was a practical, economical workhorse that stood at the opposite end of the automotive spectrum from the garish, chrome-laden, finned station wagons of the '50s and '60s.

As an unpretentious, almost anti-establishment machine, the VW van was embraced by the hippie movement of the '60s. Cheap and easy to repair, it became a kind of counter-culture car, usually decorated with pictures of flowers and phosphorescent paint.

Chrysler and others have long since taken the minivan leadership from Volkswagen. But the German firm at least has the satisfaction of knowing that it established the genre way back in 1950.

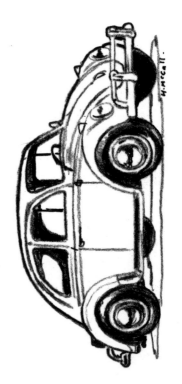

Volkswagen Beetle – Wheels for the masses

INDEX

About the author . . .

Bill Vance has had a lifelong interest in the automobile, particularly the historical and technical aspects, and has been writing about it for 25 years. His work has appeared in a wide variety of consumer, trade and technical publications in Canada and the U.S. He is an associate editor of Carguide, Canada's premier automotive magazine. Memberships include the Society of Automotive Historians, the Automobile Journalists Association of Canada, and the Periodical Writers Association of Canada. He and his wife Beth live in Rockwood, Ontario.

◆

◆

◆